T0368081

WOULDWORK

THE CARPENTER'S BLUEPRINT FOR MARRIAGE
(FOR THE MAN OF GOD)

TIMOTHY CADE

WESTBOW
PRESS®
A DIVISION OF THOMAS NELSON
& ZONDERVAN

WestBow Press books may be ordered through booksellers or by contacting:

WestBow Press
A Division of Thomas Nelson & Zondervan
1663 Liberty Drive
Bloomington, IN 47403
www.westbowpress.com
844-714-3454

ISBN: 979-8-3850-3899-2 (sc)
ISBN: 979-8-3850-3900-5 (hc)
ISBN: 979-8-3850-3901-2 (e)

Library of Congress Control Number: 2024924901

Print information available on the last page.

WestBow Press rev. date: 02/05/2025

Dedication

My Creator. My Savior. My Comforter. My God. Here am I.

Mona, as I walk out being a godly husband my hope is that every day you are reminded of what my words "thank you" cannot express.

To Hue J. Bullock, Jr., the greatest and deepest of friends one of a few I will always call 'my brother.' Your unwavering support and encouragement helped bring this book to print. Forever in my heart, Tim.

CONTENTS

PREFACE

For the past five or six years I have had a persistent feeling that I needed to write this book. Most times, when I got that feeling, I would start writing but then a few days later, *maybe* a week, I would stop. I could easily come up with any excuse to stop and sometimes I didn't even need one. Every excuse felt liberating…temporarily. Sometimes I would stop because I could never get my writing to flow as I wanted. For whatever reason (or for any reason) I could never see the process through to its completion. Weeks, months, and years at a time would go by and a part of me had no problem with that. Looking back at it, deep down I now know there were parts of me that didn't want to write this book.

I am sharing this because I want you to know I am just a regular guy. I put my pants on one leg at a time. I sometimes doubt my own value and abilities. Let me give it to you straight. I am a flawed man. I am the guy who can make the wrong turn *with* GPS! When I put on a pull–over shirt, I have a fifty–fifty chance at putting it on the right way, way too often putting it on backwards. If that weren't enough, I am not yet the perfect husband. I have experienced and caused many "bumps and bruises" in my day. Sometimes I knew what I was doing but most of the time I was absolutely clueless. I have been through a divorce. Some days I don't meet God's standard for being a husband. I sometimes feel ravaged from fighting with doing what God says, the right thing, instead of what I feel like doing. Thankfully, those days are far and few, but I still fight with them. There are significantly more good days when everything is – how do others say it? – hunky–dory? But you and I are not here because we are trying to figure out how to handle those days, when things are working like a well–oiled machine. At those times I have yet to feel the need to fall to my knees with tears flowing, lifting holy hands, effectually and fervently praying – "God I believe but help my unbelief!"

It hit me upside the head one day completely out of the blue. What I heard in my mind was *Stop listening to those excuses. Do what you have to do. Your shortcomings are not liabilities, so stop giving them so much power!*

I said all of that to make this point: presenting God's case for marriage does not require perfection from me as a husband and man of God. Sharing my personal experiences for others' sake does not necessitate having been fully complete. But that begs the question, *Why do I believe men of all ages, regardless of marital status, would benefit from hearing what I have to say about marriage?* With all that I am, I truly believe what you are about to read is spiritually educational *with* benefits felt in the physical. Men can learn a great deal about marriage from a God–fearing man/husband who is not yet perfect, is wrong sometimes, has been divorced, caused bumps and bruises, gets bumped and bruised, and is at war with himself daily because—

- My desire, more than anything else, is to remain in the will of God as a man and husband.
- I bring wisdom to this subject by way of personal experience (more than thirty years).
- I have spent countless hours in study and prayer on the subject of marriage alone.
- My compelling desire is to help other men in their walk with God and their wives (indirectly families and communities).
- God never said the road is wide, paved, a straight shot, or without obstacles.
- I am not on this earth to stand around with my hands in my pockets.

This book is not about *my* story though I include some of my experiences in this journey. This book is about what *the* author and finisher of our faith says about his men's responsibilities in marriage, point–by–point. I added wins and losses (personal and through other's experience) in certain areas for relatability. It is by God's faithfulness, mercy, and grace that I have seen great things happen in my marriage because of my obedience. Without a modicum of doubt, I believe blessings in other areas in my life came because I am faithfully working through the carpenter's blueprint for marriage in my life every day. In my humble opinion, *all* of these reasons good and bad, make me a good resource for a book like this.

I have asked myself how impactful this book would be had I not gone through all that I did. Is the best financial advisor one who doesn't have money? How about a financial advisor who is wealthy all because of an inheritance? Or is the best advisor the one who had money, made some bad investments and learned from them, and is now doing quite well? Such an advisor is doing what he or she does because he or she wants others to be wealthy without making the same mistakes. Yeah, I'll choose the latter every time. Most of those in the Bible made some bad choices and God still used them to his glory. Nah, I'm good. I've got this. God's got me.

Fairly recently I concluded that, obedience (staying in the will of God) meant I needed to complete this book. Since I had that moment of clarity my thoughts have been flowing like an open faucet, so much so that I wish my typing could keep up. I should have paid much better attention in typing class years ago. Boy, am I bad at typing (and the worst at texting)!

INTRODUCTION

I hope that this book has grabbed your attention because you are looking for something that will provide you, a man of God, with some guidance on how to live out your marriage. Or maybe you're looking because everything is good, but you are focusing more on getting things in line with what God says. I have good news, in either case I think this book will answer the call. But I am hoping this book will reach much deeper, grabbing the attention of *every* man of God, including those planning to get married at some point in the future, the divorcé, and even the widower. Men, regardless of your current marital status, I believe this book is that "something" we all need before, during, and even after marriage.

I created the following two short, bulleted lists in hopes that they will paint a quick and honest picture of what you should and should not expect from *Wouldwork The Carpenter's Blueprint For Marriage (For The Man Of God).*

What you should expect.

- This book is for men: single, engaged, married, divorced, or widowed.
- This book facilitates a deeper walk with God as it relates to marriage.
- This book helps men understand God's requirements as married men.
- This book methodically steps through the Scriptures and is easy to follow.
- This book is written for all levels of believers.
- This book is based on the word of God.

- This book is counterintuitive because it is based on many of God's principles.
- This book will challenge men wherever they are in their walk with God.

Now, what you should not expect.

- This book is not "self–help".
- This book is not unreasonable, impractical, or theoretical.
- This book is not academic, but a conversation amongst brothers.
- This book is not entirely subjective.
- This book is not easy to swallow.
- This book is not a how–to guide for "saving" a marriage.
- This book will not help you make your wife "feel" loved.
- This book will not point the finger of blame at anyone.
- This book will not directly address fatherhood or family issues.

A note for the Bible scholars: I make it my purpose to read the Bible exegetically. Admittedly though, I do take some liberties where/when a different way of looking at things may be beneficial, provided that different perspective does not impact my walk with God. For example, we can all agree that there is not a lot of information available to us with regard to creation and the fall. I do sometimes attempt to read between the lines of Genesis chapters 1 – 3 but not to the point where I purposefully or knowingly undermine his word, his wisdom, or negatively impact my walk with him. Teaching and counseling others are huge responsibilities, and both are very important to God. Consequently, I do not take either lightly. When I take any liberties in this book, I will clearly communicate something to the effect that the statement is my belief, my thought, or my opinion. I want to be clear what is scripture and what is not. Much like the clarifications Paul makes that we will look at later in this book. That way, if I am wrong everyone needs only think, *Ah, this guy's perspective may be a little different than mine (or what I am used to hearing) but there isn't anything heretical, alarming, or even concerning.*

On to another very important matter. This book does not attempt to dive too deeply into the human psyche. This author is well aware of the fact that emotions like anger, resentment, and hurt are serious problems in not only marriage but other types of relationships as well. I am aware of and acknowledge the fact that our feelings, our perceptions, and the things behind why we do the things we do are very real. If the reader is not aware of any strongholds in their life, there is a good chance that through revelation by the Spirit, this book, and self–examination, they may meet up with them face–to–face. The Holy Spirit can use the contents of this book to reveal those deeper issues. I am sure that has the potential to be scary for some, but confrontation with strongholds is an essential part of healing and correction. My advice, meet those strongholds head on and prayerfully deal with them. To those I remind, God has not given you a spirit of fear but one of power and a sound mind (2 Timothy 1:7). The spirit of love will also accompany you through this journey. However, as it relates to this book, uncovering and addressing those deeper issues is well beyond its scope. The great thing about all of this is that God's scope is without bound. He sees all, knows all, and can handle everything brought before him. In our weakness(es) he shows up strong! (2 Corinthians 12:9) There is hope!

Along that same vein, some Christians have strong opinions about believers using any resource other than God (through prayer and faith) for mental and emotional healing. For whatever it's worth, I respectfully but strongly disagree. I do not believe prayer is the *only* option, but as with everything, prayer should *always* be exercised first and on a continuous basis. I believe it is perfectly fine to talk with one or more mental health professionals whenever the need arises. Seeking help is not indicative of a lack of faith or trust in God. God has people everywhere to help *his* people anywhere. Throughout the Bible we see God healing people through other people. Why would anyone believe that stopped? That is how God seems to do a lot of what he does – through people. That is not only through the physical laying on of hands but also includes intercessory prayer. Reiterating my position, I absolutely believe that when needed, getting help is a good and responsible thing to do. It should be done in tandem with continued prayer and the exercising of faith. It is important not to neglect the latter for the former though. Our faith and trust must always be in him, not entirely in others.

This book can serve as a condensed guide for working through marriage. Essentially, it is the way God designed it long before we arrived on the scene. I previously thought and have had many men say to me, "If only there were a manual..." Well, there is one, a blueprint if you will, it just takes a little bit of effort to assemble it. God created the blueprint because he knew we would need it. He also knew that our enemy would do everything in his power to sabotage marriage. Why? I believe it is because a couple walking in his will *and* in unity have unfettered access to his supreme power.

I have unwavering belief that if men and women were to follow his blueprint, marriages "wouldwork". There would be a stark contrast between Christian marriages and those of the world. Today, that is not the case as the numbers indicate strong similarity.

If you were to look up the definition of blueprint you'd find a dizzying array of explanations. Google's Dictionary box is where I found the definition that captures the very meaning I hoped to communicate through this book's title: "a design plan".

If we were to look at a blueprint of a house, we would quickly realize that a blueprint does not provide detailed steps for building a house (or anything else). It provides a visual of the house along with important details related to its design (layout) and structure. This book contains the important details God provides us through his Son, Jesus (the master carpenter) as to the structure of marriage. God's design plan is that we love our wives as Christ loved the church (Ephesians 5:25).

FIRST THINGS FIRST

As we embark on this journey together there are some clarifying points I wish to get out and into the open. As it relates to the delivery/tone of this book, it is important that I tell you that I understand one of my, as some call it, "issues"…is that I am a very objective person. My experience has been that this way of thinking can be an issue as it seems most people either do not think or act objectively. At least not with any consistency.

The interesting conversations are the ones where subjectivity is pawned off as objectivity. Why is this so common? Is this a by–product of a clash between being Christian and moral relativism that society is trying to cram down our collective throats? I have found it to be the case that most "strange conversations" come about as a consequence of dissonance reduction. This happens when someone has two conflicting thoughts or beliefs, and they try, by whatever means, to reduce the conflict through justification gymnastics. Unfortunately, these types of conversations are not only in the world but are readily observable from those within the faith. They know what the Scriptures say to do, yet they do something entirely different. The absolutely amazing thing is they can actually rationalize it and consequently believe they are compliant!

How "emotional" the exchange gets between us really depends on how objective the other person is or where I draw a mental line in the sand. Because I have experienced this all too often on the same subjects, the line reminds me of where I need to stop because I know

1

how this story inevitably ends. Since it is impossible for me to know how objective you are, I need to explain how objective I am straight out of the gate. I am not intentionally aiming to frustrate anyone. If you find yourself getting frustrated with my delivery/tone, I sincerely apologize in advance. It is probably not you but me. But here is the cold, hard truth. In our walk with God, we *need* to be more objective because he is objective. I feel that as believers we need to hear more objective truth from one another.

I never use my objectivity of the Word of God as a means of browbeating or preaching from a soapbox. I do not see myself more pious or righteous. I use it to encourage others (as well as myself) because objectivity acts as hardened barriers keeping us on the right path. It reminds us that we can be confident that things will work out in our favor. Objectivity should not be given or taken in a disparaging manner. For those who live in a perpetual state of offense, there is no way to deliver any message that will ever satisfy them. They have to take a longer path starting with getting right with God, in which the reality of removing the constant state of offense exists. Then and only then will they ever be in a place where they can understand the benefits of correction.

When we look at the objectivity of God's Word, we will find truth irrespective of our feelings and rationalizations. The Bible is objective truth despite what the world thinks, and unfortunately, even some within the faith. Its objectivity, in all its ways, considers our human condition. Truth is, the Bible was given to us as a consequence of the human condition!

There was a time not too long ago when I believed that the reason I was created with an objective mind was to work in information technology (IT). You know how folks say that the thing that comes naturally to them is the thing they were created to do? I don't believe that, but I do believe IT is one of several career options for the objective mind. I think like a computer. Either the bit is on, or the bit is off. Either I am doing "it" or I am not doing "it." This mindset has also proven quite helpful in my walk with God. After studying the Scriptures for so many years, I now realize that I have this mind so that I can understand his Word (part of my purpose). It helps me to see what is being said, and what is not being said. I believe I have this mind because it facilitates effective Word study (2 Timothy 2:15). Of course, God also made provision for me to occupy ("do business" — NKJV) while I am here. *That* is the reason I am an IT professional, that I may occupy. With all of that in mind, I must say again that I mean no offense with the overall tone of this book should you find its objectivity offensive.

Fellas, I know by way of experience that there are times when being married can seem tough. I also know by way of experience how great it really is. But what is most important is knowing that God calls marriage "very good". Whether we are in a mountain top or a valley moment, God *still* calls it very good. I now know that my confidence in what God says about marriage allows me to experience valley moments from a bird's eye view. The more faith I gain the higher I soar above the problem.

Here is a heads–up for you. I enjoy words and I like mental imagery. But what I *really* like are words that inspire mental imagery. Before the end of the book I will use words to try to inspire you to create mental imagery. I believe that it helps things "stick" in my mind far better. Hopefully that works for you.

As men of God, he has placed commands (that is, precepts, directives, laws, etc.) before us through his Word. Starting in part four of this book we will go through those directives penned out for us to follow. Most people look at God's commands as being limiting. I disagree strongly. I find his commands to be liberating. If you are not there yet, I encourage you to get to the place where you see his commands as "a good thing".

When Adam and Eve were given their assignments, they had the liberty to do and eat whatever they chose *except* for one thing — eat the fruit from the tree of the knowledge of good and evil. In case you missed that, they had free reign except for *one* thing that they were not permitted to do. If God didn't put at least one thing they could not do, then there is no option but to obey. Free will cannot exist where there is not a choice to be made. Said differently, they could only obey, and it would not be a conscious free–will choice. God wants it so that we obey him because we choose to, not because no alternative exists.

Imagine walking into your local grocery store and the only thing you see are white cans with the label that read "Beans". Aisle after aisle, shelf after shelf, nothing but beans. *That,* my friend, is an example of *restrictive.* Now add one aisle of corn. Suddenly there is liberty. You can choose one or the other. Restrictive is the removal of the ability to choose between at least two things by allowing only one.

Apparently not being able to eat from every tree was too restrictive in the eyes of Eve and Adam. The irony in that is that when you talk to most believers today about this subject, they're quick to say that they wouldn't have eaten the fruit of the forbidden tree. As they are talking to me I guess they don't realize that they're picking the skin of the forbidden fruit from between their teeth. I'm not stirring up these conversations — people come to me with them. I do offer a helping hand, but most seem not to make the effort to reach for it being satisfied with playing the "grace card."

The reality of the situation then and now is like two sides of the same coin: Adam and Eve's choice is no different than ours. Our choice is no different from Adam and Eve's. The sad part is that we know the consequence of their decision and still make the same bold choices we make. We do not see the list of exclusions as being the noise that they truly are. Everything God provides is freeing, not restrictive. Imagine cracking open a brand–new board game, opening the board, the pieces, the cards, and such — then asking out loud after realizing there are instructions (even before actually reading them), "Why is this game so restrictive?" I have found that most people don't even know what the rules are but nevertheless call this walk restrictive. Oh, I should have clarified — people in the church do this!

In this book we will go through all the ordinances that God provides men with as they pertain to marriage. These are liberties and they are light especially when contrasted with the weight of any of the alternatives actually available to us, the alternatives being those things that don't make his list of liberties. So much mess comes with choosing otherwise — imaginable consequences (you know — those that we say, "won't happen to me!") as well as the unimaginable.

As we go through them, please hold onto these words:

> If you abide in Me, and My words abide in you, you
> will ask what you desire, and it shall be done for you.

> By this My Father is glorified, that you bear much fruit;
> so you will be My disciples. As the Father loved Me,
> I also have loved you; abide in My love. If you keep
> My commandments, you will abide in My love, just as
> I have kept My Father's commandments and abide in
> His love. These things I have spoken to you, that My
> joy may remain in you, and that your joy may be full.
> This is My commandment, that you love one another
> as I have loved you. (John 15:7–12 NKJV)

These verses so neatly dovetail into one of my other favorites, from the previous chapter: "If you love Me you will keep my commandments" (John 14:15). Too many in the faith shirk the believer's responsibility to abide by God's commandments (the law of Christ). They often rebut, "The new covenant is about relationship, not religious rules. Following rules is legalistic." Oh really? Riddle me this: How exactly does one go about having a relationship (a good one, of course) with someone all the while operating without the consideration of the person he or she hopes to relate to?

If you have kids, you may have an easier time with the following example. If you do not have children, stretch your imagination here — it's an easy one. Two parents have two children. One does everything in opposition to the established order. The other child does everything well within the lines. Both children are consistent in their respective behavior. While I agree that neither parent should love one child over the other, I might even go as far as saying that any one child should not be a favorite of either parent. Which child would have the better relationship with his or her parents?

Let's make it personal. Suppose you have established rules for driving the car: Mind the speed limit. No texting or talking on the cell phone. No more than one other passenger. Fill up the gas tank before you park it at home. How would you respond to the child who abides by those rules when borrowing the car versus the one who has a stack of speeding tickets and on many different occasions has been spotted with numerous other kids in the car, allowing two of them to hang out the window and the sunroof while the car is in motion? How long will the one who abides by the rules keep doing so if there is no recourse meted out to the rule–breaking sibling? If I were a betting man I would stack my money on the relationship with the obedient child being more positive over the relationship with the rebellious child. In my mind I can imagine that the two relationships *must* be different.

What would this look like if this were friendship? Can you disregard what friendship means to the person you wish to befriend? How about in a marriage? I hope my point is made by way of these few examples.

Here is a truth — one cannot walk in the God kind of love without first being saved and having the indwelling of the Holy Spirit. The two open the door to the possibility of living with his kind of love. In order to actually walk it out, obedience (carrying of the cross and dying to self daily) is essential. Enoch would chime in and call it "walking with God".

The commands for the married man that we will go over in part four of this book are outlined so that we know what they are and are better able to walk in them — first, because it is commanded, second, because God is glorified through our obedience in them, and finally, because it comes with some really cool perks! We want to abide in him where there is peace and safety. We want our prayers answered. We want our joy full. In the event that does not yet resonate, let's try its inverse. If we do not do these things, we will not be where there is peace and safety. We will not get our prayers answered and our joy will be lacking.

No need to scour the entire Bible — I have everything collected here so that all you need to do is read this and find its references in your Bible. Like Scrubbing Bubbles, I worked hard so you don't have to. Before we dive in together, I want to explain what I mean by "walk with God" as I use it often throughout this book and because others use the phrase differently.

When I use "walk with God," it is figurative language used as representation of one's conduct. I mean striving for the type of walk that the Bible explicitly notes two people accomplished: Enoch, walked with God 300 years (Genesis 5:22,24), and Noah (Genesis 6:9) was a righteous man, blameless in the time he walked with God. Of course, Jesus walked with God by doing what he saw the Father do and nothing more as he tells us in John 5:19. Also, through his directive to follow him (Matthew 19:21), walking with God is made clear.

Unfortunately for me, being a task list–oriented kind of guy, I realize that we are not given detail as to how we are able to become a member of this elite group. Just because the Bible mentions only two does not imply no one else did or that it is not something anyone else can accomplish. I see it as an opportunity to join an elite group. In almost all that I do, I think, *Why not go for it?* And while I am going for it, I also think that I want to be really good at it. Being able to do something is rarely ever where it ends with me. This mentality is not limited to the "big things." It is one of the precipitating thoughts behind most of my off–the–wall accomplishments. I know I'm not the only guy thinking like this. If that were so, YouTube how–to videos would *never* have taken off. I have done many things just because someone else was able to do it. On the flip side, I have also gotten myself into a mess for the very same reason! That won't happen with us here because God is behind us in every facet of our spiritual growth and walk with him!

This book is different in that it does not come up with some new way of doing things. It returns us to God's blueprint for marriage before man was ever created, a foolproof method of how marriage should be done. Permit me to explain by way of example as it helps me to deliver the point I am trying to make when my direct explanation can be a little technical and dry. I blame that on being an IT guy.

There's always a book that provides some level of success in marriage. To the authors who have toiled to get their books on marriage to print in an effort to help those in need: thank you. They can definitely be helpful. But the book must be firmly rooted in the will of God. Most have nothing to do with the will of God as it relates to marriage. Marital statistics have been proving for numerous decades that "something else" is needed.

Thank you for your patience, now let's begin.

This may come as a shock to you, but let the record state, "You were made for marriage." It is important that you really try to understand those words. God purposed it from before creation for you to be joined in marriage with one woman.

Whether you are single, married, or divorced. God created marriage to maximize men's and women's potential alike, making the two entirely complete in him. Together, you and I are going to methodically step through all of his precepts on marriage. If you are not a man of God (by that I mean a born–again, Holy Spirit–filled Christian) this book is of no use to you. You cannot sift out the "God parts" and have the rest work in a secular marriage. Neither will this work for the "Sunday–only Christian." The creator did not design his plan for marriage to work that way. And his way is the perfect way. In similar fashion, the creator of the remote control for your brand of television set did not purpose it to work on any other brand of television set. Surely you're not mad at him or her for that! What God has to say about his men and marriage is vitally important and its promises are not universally applicable.

This book is scripturally based. Yet it is not so spiritual that it loses any reasonableness and practicality. I am not making up the "rules" — God did, and he is not unreasonable or impractical! Like a challenging puzzle, as we lay down the pieces you will see God's picture of marriage and how we fit in that picture. I should note for those who prefer a step–by–step process to follow (me!), this process is not like that. I cannot and would not promise that if you follow some set of steps, you will have success. If only there was a step–by–step guide, right? There isn't. But we will put together the ingredients. With that, if you are diligent about obedience, I am confident that your walk with him will be successful. In fact, I will take it one step further. As you develop and strengthen your walk with God, your other relationships will also be positively impacted almost by default (that is, with little added effort).

Although this book is heavily scriptural, you do not need to be a Bible expert. This is slow and easy to follow. While you should have your Bible with you, I do provide many verses that can be read in line with the book. I don't want to give them all to you as my way of encouraging you to dig in. While I prefer to use the New American Standard Bible (NASB) or the New King James Version (NKJV), I do use others. You should always feel free to read the version you are most comfortable with. My thought is this: if you cannot understand it, how can it possibly be of any use to you?

Reiterating, this is not an easy walk. But that should not be taken to mean that this walk is an impossible one. I will not suggest there won't be let downs or periods of frustration. It is our nature that is exclusively responsible for making this walk challenging. Paul's words should remind us that this walk involves mind–renewing (Romans 12:2). When you compound that with someone else's contributions, it becomes even more challenging. During those times when you are feeling discouraged, I include a number of my favorite encouraging verses in section V hoping that they help you to keep pressing. Always remember that despite the challenges the reward is too great to quit! Here are a few recommendations I came up with to help you get the most out of this book.

1. Whether it be a Bible app or hard copy, have your Bible handy. Regardless of what you're reading or who it is from, you always want to know what the Word of God says, not just what someone else tells you it says.
2. Before you start reading any faith–based book, pray for God's revelation, wisdom, understanding, and discernment. Be sincere and transparent with your prayers. Share your innermost thoughts and feelings with God. You are not surprising him in any way by what you say. We are not always aware of the motives behind our actions (that is, what's going on in the heart). God knows you and your heart — intimately.
3. God knows what marriage is supposed to look like. He created it. He has it optimized so that the parts are made to fit one another only one way. What I am alluding to is this: Put your marriage together the way God designed it. Do not allow your inclinations and proclivities to have any influence on your doing marriage his way.

Imagine that you have been given an assignment: You must put together a bookcase as it has been on the "honey–do list" for far too long. You could just tear into the box and try putting it together based on the picture on the outside of the box. Or you could put it together based on the instructions the manufacturer provided. While you could spend time trying to figure out why you don't like to follow instructions (learned behavior, you prefer to figure it out, and so on), the best way, all things being equal, is to follow the manufacturer's method for putting it together. The manufacturer knows what the product is supposed to look like and how it functions best. The manufacturer knows what parts are included. God is the manufacturer of marriage. We must follow his instruction.

IN *THE* BEGINNING

We should all be quite familiar with Adam and Eve and the fall, so I won't go into the story in its entirety here. I would, however, like to point out a few things.

> And the LORD God said, "It is not good that man should be alone; I will make him a helper comparable to him." Out of the ground the LORD God formed every beast of the field and every bird of the air, and brought them to Adam to see what he would call them. And whatever Adam called each living creature, that was its name. So Adam gave names to all cattle, to the birds of the air, and to every beast of the field. But for Adam there was not found a helper comparable to him. And the LORD God caused a deep sleep to fall on Adam, and he slept; and He took one of his ribs, and closed up the flesh in its place. Then the rib which the LORD God had taken from man He made into a woman, and He brought her to the man. (Genesis 2:18–22 NKJV)

Here are some of my notes from these five verses:

- It is not good for man to be alone.
- God made a helper for man because out of all his previous creation, none was found.

- God created woman from part of the man not from the ground as was everything else before her.
- Woman was comparable!

Reassembling with a little paraphrasing, God created man but he was alone. God looked at man's condition at that time and said that being alone was not good. To show man that nothing else would resolve this predicament, he then created all land and flying animals. Don't miss the point. God was not experimenting. He knew what man needed. He was showing man (Adam — and us) that nothing else would do!

You see, this is why it is entirely possible to be a single Christian (or married but outside his will) with our days, weeks, and months filled with all sorts of things yet unable to shake the feeling of being incomplete. We can have a few close friends or several circles of many friends. It will not change the condition. It is because we are disconnected from our mates and by default our purpose and the will of God. Some may or may not realize this problem, but it leads to trying to fill incompleteness with all sorts of things to keep "busy." The reprieve is only temporary. The hole is still there, and nothing is satisfying it — inevitably leading to more "stuff." That thing being sought after — it's not a hobby. It's not a job. It's not a friend or relative. We are wasting unrecoverable time trying to fill a void where *nothing* else is designed or ordained to fit.

Perhaps that is just not clicking yet. I'm writing to a wide audience with all of us in various places in our lives. So let me try it this way. For those of us who lived any considerable time before coming to the Lord, you should be able to connect with my point more readily. Remember when you did those things that you needed to be "saved" from? You know, those things that no matter how much you did it, they were just not enough? Or you graduated onto things that were progressively "higher" only to discover that they were not enough either? Something was missing. It did not matter what you filled that emptiness with or how much of how many different things — they were not filling the void. They were successful at keeping you busy. My, and what a busy calendar you had! Well, the hole you had that only God could fill is remarkably like the hole you have for a God–created suitable mate, your complementary wife!

Husbands, get this. The very same hole we have, our wives have as well. It is not just for a man's experience. Think about it. How reasonable would it be for God to create a void in you only for her while she was entirely complete in and of herself? That's not reasonable. He didn't. We must stop thinking our wives don't need us. We must stop thinking we are but accessories. When we shake that thought, that's the moment we can become who we were meant to be: the man of God, for God, for her, not to mention our families and communities. Remember from this point forward that God created her for you and you for her. Together you are to become one (complete).

Next, God did not say "Let us allow man to create his own helper." *God* made his helper. From that it is reasonable to conclude that man was incapable of creating his own. Or just for argument, even if he could, he didn't even know what he needed. God took the responsibility upon himself to create what man needed. He knew exactly what man needed and where his need would be sourced — from within him.

Man of God, our suitable helper is not our favorite sports team. Our suitable helper is not our buddies from college. It is not a woman outside of the one we married. It is not found in our fishing trips with the guys. God created woman, and she is perfectly designed to do exactly what it is that she was created to do with us. She is all and exactly what we need. And let me state this now for the record — she may not have been created to do what *we* want her to do, depending on what that want is!

Moving along —

> And Adam said: "This is now bone of my bones And flesh of my flesh; She shall be called Woman, Because she was taken out of Man." Therefore a man shall leave his father and mother and be joined to his wife, and they shall become one flesh. (Genesis 2:23–24 NKJV)

For some this may be a hard pill to swallow, but it must be said. It is improper for a man to be attached to his parents — yes, that includes Mom. As such, it is also improper that a woman be attached to *her* parents. This is in the marriages in which the parent has control over a marriage partner and in effect can manipulate what takes place in the marriage for their benefit. This is ungodly! God designed marriage partners to become one. We cannot be equally attached to our wives and to our parents at the same time. Jesus said it is not possible to serve two masters because, we will be devoted to one and despise the other (Matthew 6:24; Luke 16:13). Just to be clear, this excludes the care of sick and/or elderly parents, but we should stay vigilant that we do not leave ourselves vulnerable or in a position to be manipulated. Remember that we are to honor our parents, not to dishonor them. Furthermore, there are numerous scriptures that require care and love of others. However, there is no gray area between caring for, having love for, and attachment. Moving on —

> God saw all that he had made, and behold, it was very good. And there was evening and there was morning, the sixth day. Thus, the heavens and the earth were completed, and all their hosts. By the seventh day God completed his work which he had done. (Genesis 1:31–2:2 NKJV)

In several places throughout this book I have a few key images that are metaphorical representations of different stages in life, particularly married life. There are also a few fictional snippets found in this book. Their purpose is to stimulate your imagination and provoke thought relating to the complexities of married life. The fictional accounts are in italicized typeface to help differentiate them from the rest of the biblically based work. Here is the first one:

Today is my twenty-second day away at college. It is just as overwhelming today as it was on day one. There are so many different people from so many different places, not just from the United States but worldwide. I still feel a bit unsettled, though not fearful anymore.

Just as in high school, there are pockets of people groups scattered about. This place is huge. I am still trying to navigate the grounds, though I am getting lost a little less. Mom and Dad were right again—this place is big. I thought I wanted big after coming from such a small city. I should have gone to a smaller school. My classes have hundreds of students in them. I have yet to meet my professor. Well . . . it is what it is at this point. It's only four years, right?

As I walk back to my dorm room from class, weaving in and out of cliquey groups, I miss knowing people. I miss being home. I miss the food. I miss my bed! All of my snarky comments to others in anticipation of finally being on my own are turning out not to be what I thought. Am I free? Yes. But there are no bounds . . . at all! Well, except for the fact that I am, well, essentially broke. So I guess there are some confines.

Finally at my dorm. Every corridor I walk through or pass reminds me of the prison shows on TV, except that these walls are brightly painted cinderblock instead of the prison's defaulted gray. Oh, and of course, anywhere there is wall space you find flyers for parties and clubs, announcements for one Greek organization or another, notices of books for sale, or anything else imaginable and unimaginable. Welcome signs, names, pictures are plastered across most dorm room doors—except for a few naked doors, of which mine is one. I am not really creative and definitely not artistic. My door looks as if the room is still eagerly awaiting its new residents. Or, as is my case, weird people dwell within.

I drop my stuff onto the commercial earth-toned carpet tiles and flop onto my unmade bed—one freedom I have come to appreciate! Aside from my unkempt bed, oh, and my roommate, this room is so sterile compared to the open-door rooms I passed along the way. No memories or photos of favorite music groups adorn these walls.

I tire myself of just contemplating how much time I have left. Yeah, I guess I see this, again like prison, as a bid. I have four years to do. If this is going to get any better, I might as well join in the crowd. But for now I am just going to rest a little. My roomie isn't here and most students on my floor are out and about. Solace.

I lie on my side looking out the window, an hour and a half before my next class Psych, 120 kids deep. Ugh! It feels as if my body is growing exponentially heavier. Looking beyond the cloudy pane of glass, too high to see anything but the canopy of the tallest trees and the blue sky, I can no longer hold open my heavy eyelids. Yeah, I am going to sleep, indicative of that indescribable feeling of falling into my mattress.

"You know, Tim, college life is going to be one of your favorite and most memorable experiences," says a stranger. And had he not said "Tim," I most certainly would have looked around for confirmation that he was speaking to me.

"Is that right?" I respond, draped with sarcasm.

"Definitely. Just give it a little time. I promise: one day you are going to hate to leave this place."

"Yeah, okay." Again, it's as sarcastic as I can muster up. Wait—that sounds as though I had to dig down deep in an effort to find some sarcasm. Nope. No digging necessary. It lay right on top, nice and thick, in fact. "And how would you know that?"

"He told me to tell you."

"He . . . told you . . . to tell me?" I ask, pointing at each of our chests in time to be sure there is no confusion. "And who is 'he'?"

"God. Our creator."

"Right! God. Sure. Our creator. And who are you?"

"My name is Anthoniel." He responds with a dash of charm, wit, and personality.

What is with this guy? Where on earth am I? And again, who is this guy?

"He sent me to show you some things, and it is not really where you are but when you are. I am your guardian angel."

Did I say that out loud? Thinking. I am sure, more accurately, still thinking.

"Okay. Make sense to me. Anthoniel, my guardian angel, sent to talk to me by God our creator." As I start walking in the opposite direction from where I was going, I have no idea where—but as long as this character is no longer in my personal space, I'm good. So wherever he is not works for me.

Now a few purposefully brisk paces away, I look up—and he's right in front of me. Yeah, that was weird or perhaps he's just fast. I don't know, but either way I need to keep it moving. I'll head this way, again, somewhere he is not because not only is he talking weird, but he's also got some stalking issue or something.

"Wait!" he commands. All charm and personality having disappeared without a trace. He also looks different. Bigger? Stronger? I can't place it. Something about him is definitely different.

Okay, I thought he was weird but suddenly everything around us stops. Now, this is definitely weird! Not a single sound. Not the squawk of a bird nor the beep of a car's horn. Not even the gratuitous barking dog that's in the background of every single movie or show that's heard. Yeah, I am a little frazzled.

"You need to listen. I must show you something. I have things to talk with you about."

I can't exactly say he had me at "Hello," but now I can definitely say with surety that he has my undivided attention. I am all ears. As I look around, the bright, what I thought should be an unseasonably warm fall day, begins losing its color and simultaneously fades, surrendering itself to absolute darkness. You know—the kind of darkness you experience because you cannot see it. The kind of darkness that carries its own weight as proof of its existence. Well past the windowless-basement-after-someone-accidently-turns-off-the-light-and-closes-the-door-thinking-no-one-is-down-there darkness. Oddly, I'm cool with it. If it were not for him, I could be terrified right now.

"Watch," he demands.

Okay, so I am not exactly sure what there is to see because I cannot see the tip of my tongue. Yeah, I know because I tried. Suddenly off in the great distance I see something. Squinting, I cannot make it out. Okay, I now see more of it. It looks like . . . maybe a doghouse. No, a shed. It is not because my vision is adjusting that the picture is coming clearer,—it is because it is moving toward us at blistering speed. As I describe what I see, it is becoming more apparent what it is not because it's closer than when I thought I recognized what it was. It is coming so fast that it sounds like gale—no storm, no hurricane-force wind. Suddenly it is right in front of us and immediately stops. Voom! It is a house.

Admittedly, I am thinking in my usually sarcastic tone, "Quite a bit of dramatics for a house! And why couldn't we just walk or drive to it?"

"Silence." Again I wonder, "Did I say that out loud?"

"This was you."

In my head I see nothing but question marks everywhere but taking care not to say a word.

"When you were born into this world our Father provided you with everything you needed: a clean heart and spirit. You were blameless, spotless. You were trusting. You would be perfectly loving. This house is a visual representation of your heart and mind. Let's go inside."

Immediately we begin moving toward the house, but my legs are absolutely still. It's getting closer. Closer. I ball up, expecting to smack into the house, never once thinking that we would travel through its exterior. Okay, new level of weird here. We are standing inside. "Well, that was pretty cool actually" I think as I look at my extremities, trying to figure out if that was real.

He continues: "Notice there are no interior walls. This space has an open floor plan. It's wide open and airy. The windows are large, letting in lots of sun. It is warm. It is clean. It is perfect and made for you by God."

As I look around, mouth agape, I cannot help but notice the perfect detail. Everything I like is here. Exterior walls—perfect. Kitchen—perfect. Color paint—perfect. No dust. I know, because I am touching everything. Well, he did say it was mine.

Growing up, I never saw a house like this. Yeah, I am sure rich people's homes looked like this, but rich I was not. Apparently though, God is, and he did this all for me. Okay, now I am running around touching everything and acting a bit giddy.

"Come," *he says invitingly.*

Just as we came in, we would exit. Through the drywall, insulation, studs, oriented strand board, house wrap, then siding. I was still in the position of opening a kitchen cabinet when suddenly I am outside, still in the "open cabinet" position.

"This is what you started with. This is where you are now. Watch."

Now the day seems to be progressing to dusk, evening, night. Now twilight, dawn, day. Over and over. Faster and faster. As I watch what looks like time passing, I get confirmation from my house as it changes with the days, months, seasons, and presumably years. It starts showing wear. In some of the windows I watch drapes magically appear and unfurl. Peering through the now dustier windows, I see walls and doors where there was only open space earlier. Yeah, not quite as pretty. Then it stops.

"This is your current mental and emotional state because of your life experiences. Walls now surround fears, worries, and shame you've developed over time. I cannot help you in dealing with these things, but there is one who can. He is the Holy Spirit. He may not present himself to you as did I, but you need to remember that he is ever present. He will show you all things as they pertain to life and godliness. Be receptive to his guidance. Remember these things. I will see you again soon."

Before I could say a word, I feel the inescapable pull of something. I cannot fight against it. I am being snatched in.

"Wham!" *Or so it feels. Squinting against the glare of the sun beaming through the window, I see the dimly lit but unmistakable figure of my roommate. What a strange dream! I look at the clock. I'm jolted upright by the realization that I have ten minutes to get to class, which is a fifteen-minute walk from my room. Great. I grab my bag and out the door I go.*

I will refer to this imagery in other places in this book as we methodically plod through God's commands for living more Christlike in our walk as husbands.

Home of the single man.

CALLING ALL...

SINGLE MEN

So, you are looking to get married? Here's the thing — when a serious conversation about marriage takes place, two things should happen: (1) you invite her into your home to look around and (2) she invites you into her home to look around.

YOUR VISIT TO HER HOUSE. As the single man, you must not just stand outside admiring the view. That is not *the* most important part of her. Time and circumstances will begin to wear on those. And yes, time and circumstances will wear on you too! Instead, through conversation, go inside don't sit down and watch TV (the replaying of her memories through story)! Ask questions. Look around. What is this house built on? What doors are locked? How many rooms are there? What does this switch do? What about that button? Don't just look at the surfaces. Get down on the floor. What's under the bed? People love to hide stuff in all sorts of strange places.

You should understand something very important. She will probably open doors only if asked. So be sure to ask. She may avoid letting you in certain rooms and that makes sense. Make note of the boundaries. Trust takes time to build and not everyone is deserving of another's trust. Over time you will need to prove yourself worthy of being let inside. But once proven, the chances are good that some of the walls will come down. Hopefully all the doors will unlock, if only for you.

Take care not to violate that trust. Otherwise they may all close, never again to be open by you, maybe anyone.

HER VISIT TO YOUR HOUSE. In likewise fashion, you should freely and willingly allow her into your house. Allow her to walk around and ask questions. Again, you don't need to divulge everything on the spot, but the idea is that over time, you will be able to remove some walls and window coverings. All this stuff was never meant to be here in the first place. Just as you want to help her, you should allow her to help you. This is one of many things husbands and wives are made to do for each other.

That is in the ideal world. Unfortunately, this is not what usually takes place. You invite someone over but both of you spend way too much time walking around outside the house, giving and receiving compliments about its color and build. Some time is spent inside, not to freely explore but instead, to be taken on a tour, walking past locked doors as if they were not even there. Settling in on the guided tour, there are things that go by completely unnoticed or unaddressed. Later this will likely come back to bite as you find out you really didn't take the time to learn all that you could and should have — of course, leading to shock when these things "show up," seemingly out of the blue.

Again, I stress that not everyone deserves to know everything right away. Some things can be shared only with others with whom we have the most intimate relationship. It's not necessarily done to be secretive. Imagine going on a first date and being pummeled with every dark detail of someone's life. A few minutes of that and, as in the movies, she will "visit" the ladies' room never to return. It works in reverse too. "Touring" too aggressively will be off-putting for sure.

Guys, as single men, this is the time to find out as much as you can about her. There is some immediate reward in this, but this investment will yield compounded interest in the future. Be patient. Be observant. Be sure to remember what you discover! You must also do the same for her. Believe it or not, while it is beneficial for her, it is also beneficial for you. You want to be with someone who is willing to put in the work with you to remove the walls you know shouldn't be there. You may not know that some rooms exist because you avoid that part of the house altogether. You want to trust, and have it not wasted on someone who does not value that. This is the time to find out if she is (or can be) that person. Can you be that person for her? Now is the time to understand that marriage is not at all about what you can get. In fact, as the husband you must have the mindset that you will be carrying most of the weight.

Above all else, you should most definitely be looking for a woman of God. If you have a true woman of God, there should be nothing the two of you cannot accomplish together in him. And by woman of God, I mean more than just going to church. Even if a woman volunteers in some capacity, that doesn't necessarily indicate that she is God-fearing. Don't get me wrong. Thoughtful is great—but saved and thoughtful is better!

So I guess I can sum it up this way: You want to select from God-fearing, churchgoing, and trustworthy women. While you wait on her, continue working on yourself. There are numerous precepts scattered throughout the Bible for single men. Of course, this book will get your mind and heart trained to be the husband of God you need to become for her. Make time for moments of self-reflection; spend time walking around your own home. You may be surprised by what you find. What work do you need to do? Everyone has something he or she could or should be doing.

I often hear people say they are better off alone. They will use the following statements from Paul as justification for their view. So, let's talk about that before we continue on with the rest of the book. I will not include all of his writing here but only the relevant parts.

- Are you free from such a commitment [marriage]? Do not look for a wife" (1 Corinthians 7:27 NIV).
- "I would like you to be free from concern. An unmarried man is concerned about the Lord's affairs—how he can please the Lord. But a married man is concerned about the affairs of this world—how he can please his wife— and his interests are divided. I am saying this for your own good, not to restrict you, but that you may live in a right way in undivided devotion to the Lord" (1 Corinthians 7:32–35 NIV).
- "So then, he who marries the virgin does right, but he who does not marry her does better" (1 Corinthians 7:38 NIV).

Whoa! Sounds as if Paul is vehemently against marriage! His view of marriage differs from God's view—that it is not good for man to be alone. What is going on here? Let's dive into this a little together to see if we can make sense of it all.

First, Paul opens this topic with a noteworthy statement: "Now about virgins: I have no command from the Lord, but I give a judgment as one who by the Lord's mercy is trustworthy" (1 Corinthians 7:25 NIV). Following that statement, we should understand that Paul is offering his personal opinion, not a command. Another important consideration regards the historical circumstances surrounding his letter to the church at Corinth. Doing so will provide us with greater contextual understanding. From Paul's writings we know that he believed Jesus would be returning within his lifetime. Paul is intimately aware of Jesus's conversation with his disciples on the Mount of Olives. He is keenly aware of the Old Testament prophecies of the end times. Intense and pervasive persecution (torture and death) of Jews and Christians will happen under Nero's direction. Although Paul wouldn't live to see it, soon the temple will be decimated (Matthew 24:1–2). If interested in reading more, The Antiquities of the Jews, by Flavius Josephus, is an excellent and very detailed resource (quite lengthy).

Suppose today you believe, because of the words of numerous prophets of God spoken years ago, that your country would suffer a massive invasion. This invasion would be unlike anything in history. Do not think of a random country, but the worse possible country you can imagine. Although there are many historical examples, use Jewish historical atrocities as a reference. Think of Israel's past invasions, persecutions, being taken into captivity, forced labor, and the many assaults against its women and children. Throw in the Nazis, when Jews were murdered by the millions, tortured, raped, forced into hard labor, robbed of everything, and such. What advice would you give to those that are unaware of or are not concerned about this prophesied incursion but are more concerned about getting married and having a family? Would you suggest that it would be wise to wait things out? How long should they wait? What should they do about their sexual, emotional, and physical desires?

Real world — I have had people say to me that they are not going to make any large purchases until interest rates come down. For some a large purchase was a new refrigerator for their kitchen. If we can feel that way about incidental things, imagine Paul's state of mind. Paul was not advising the people at a time when life was considered "normal." He felt the imminence of very difficult times. This is the context behind Paul suggesting that single people should remain single. Or more directly, as he said it this way too, not to get married. It would be better in what he felt were the last days to remain single and be fully devoted to the Lord. Yet still he says it again: "If his passions are too strong and he feels he ought to marry, he should do as he wants. He is not sinning. They should get married." (1 Corinthians 7:36 NIV)

At this point we should be able to say, with confidence, that Paul's words did not contradict God's words. They were purely circumstantial. While it is true that a married couple can become more focused on pleasing one another than God, it does not mean it must be the case. I will argue many times in this book, in marriage, that a man and woman wholly devoted to God first will be wholly devoted to one another as the two cannot be separated. We will see later that God makes provision for that. God does not demand 100 percent from man and woman *while* setting standards for the two to live out the fullest marriage. If he wanted 100 percent there would be no marriage standard because relationships would violate his will.

I have had men tell me that they accept being single in life because of what Paul said. Some actually have no idea what Paul said but believe they are better off alone — when in fact, both of us know they would rather be with someone than be alone. None of that is opinion as it is based squarely on their demeanor when they make such a statement (disappointment, acquiescence). Also, I know they try repeatedly to find someone but have not been successful. In other words, put bluntly, they have given up on the idea of finding "a good thing" for very different reasons. Usually there's something "broken" they cannot or will not fix. Another consideration is that the time alone is not used for greater devotion to God, but other things, the freedom to do whatever they want whenever they want.

Single men, it is not good for you to be alone. A piece of you, your help, is out there and she is missing something too—you. Use this time to work on yourself and your commitment to God. This will expedite his making sure you cross paths with his daughter. Know that she is out there because God created her expressly for you. When your paths collide, you will know she is the one. Again, it is not expressly based on your "Mrs. Right" qualities, but God's first and foremost.

This book will provide insight into the requirements God has for you as it pertains to marriage, starting you off in the best position for earlier and greater success in it.

MARRIED MEN

I just slid into bed five minutes ago, exhausted from a long day. After a little fidgeting and squirming, I have finally nestled into that "sweet spot," that perfect place where I know this is the last thing I will remember, the last movement I will consciously make before waking in the morning. I have no idea at this moment, but tonight is not going to be one of those "usual" nights.

Suddenly, as I look around, I realize that I am standing in . . . well . . . nothingness. Am I dreaming? What is this place? Where am I?

Out of nowhere a familiar voice beckons, "Come with me. I must show you the things that will soon take place."

The voice itself is terrifying in its vastness yet comforting in its closeness at the same time. I know this voice! I don't step in any direction but close my eyes and fall to my face immediately. I don't know why, because there is no time for any consideration to have taken place. I just fall.

Although still face-down on . . . well . . . nothing, my stomach is telling me, "We're moving!" But where am I going? Still, I feel nothingness, a place completely devoid of life.

The voice orders, "Rise!"

In obedience I stand as was commanded. I know my eyes are open. Nevertheless, I strain with every fiber of my being to open them anyway, to see anything. But there is nothing. I can't sense anything but the presence of "something," that something with the booming voice.

I know. I remember from many years ago!

That voice surrounds me, seems to hold me, keeping me suspended, but somehow I am standing in the vastness of nothingness. As nothingness presses against my skin and body, I can perceive its indescribable density, not unlike the feeling of hot, humid air pressing against the skin, but without the hot, uncomfortable feeling. Nothingness is just here . . . and not here at the same time.

My heart is racing. I can hear the beat of my own pulse in my ears. No. I don't just hear it—I feel it, the rhythmic, faint beat like from that of a very large subwoofer at a concert hall but without any other frequencies.

"Fear not. I AM has sent me to you. I must show you the things that are soon to come," he proclaims.

Admittedly, hearing "fear not" doesn't assuage my fears to any measurable degree, though I make every effort to calm myself. Suddenly, a man or what looks like a man is standing next to me, absolutely huge and in great physical shape, definitely someone or something not to be messed with.

Interrupting my thoughts, he barks, "Behold!" Pointing and looking down, I follow his finger. Look at what? I see nothing but absolute blackness. Out of the blue, my inside voice screams, "That's Anthony! No . . . wait. Is it . . . Antonio? No, that's not right either."

Off in the immeasurable distance I see something. Whatever it is, I can tell it is coming toward me with incredible speed. I remember this from years ago! Am I dreaming again? I can hear what sounds like a mixture of a very deep hum with the movement of air.

As it gets closer, I cannot make out what I am looking at. But whatever it is, just as before, it is coming at us very quickly. Wait—or am I moving down toward it? I feel as if I might be moving. Whichever the case, something is moving very fast! That much I am sure of.

I can make out what looks like the top of a house. The rhythmic pulsation in my ears and throughout my body is calming. The roaring, deep hum is quieting, along with the sound of moving air.

Voom! We stop. Or did it stop?

It is my house from the previous dream. Suspended by the same forces that keep me afloat, in absolute stillness it hovers motionless in the middle of nothingness.

Now that it is right in front of me, I can see that this is not exactly the same as it was in my earlier vision, definitely of little resemblance to the very first image I had gotten many years ago. There have been some structural changes. Through its windows I can make out pictures hanging from walls that weren't there before. There is a fence where there wasn't one before. I convince myself it only makes sense that it (me) would have undergone some change since the last time.

"Look to your right," says the massive angelic being. "What do you see?"

"I don't see any—" *I start to reply, but before I could finish, it begins again, the deep hum and the sound of moving air. This time there is no fear. But instead* of in the center of nothingness in front of me, it is at the center of nothingness to my right, a very faint light.

Again, a random thought pops into my mind: "Anthoniel! His name is Anthoniel!"

Off in a great distance, appears to be another house. In the same way as before, this house is rushing toward me at breakneck speed. The sounds increase. I can make out a house. I was right—obviously not mine, but whose?

I recognize it now. It belongs to my fiancé. I've been inside, many times. It continues to move toward us with incredible speed. It doesn't seem to be slowing down as I shift my eyes to my house, just off to the left. Uneasiness sets in. Her house needs to slow down! I shift my eyes back to her house. It shows no signs of slowing.

I respond to Anthoniel, "It looks like my fiancée's house."

As it continues moving closer, I can make out the left exterior side and most of the front. I can see the garage door. It's coming too fast. Her house is not going to stop before crashing into mine. Judging by its distance to my house, hers is now probably a few hundred feet away, still zipping along. It is not stopping. I close my eyes and cover my head and the rest of my body with my arms. I contort my body in an instinctive but vain effort to protect myself from the ensuing damage from the collision. I am too close!

He says, "Look! You will not be harmed. You must remember all that you see."

The moment I open my eyes, "Boom!" They collide. Twisting, breaking, crunching, and shattering are heard with incredible detail, so clear, as if it is taking place all around me, as if I am sitting inside the eye of the storm. A massive plume of dust is right in front of me, yet I feel nothing. Not a fleck of glass comes into contact with me, not even a splinter! But this is happening right in front of me. How is this possible? Immediately after the collision, what I feel I can only describe as a massive push of air. It is pushing against me from the front with enough force to drive me backward, perhaps several feet, but it's only a guess.

Now with the two houses in their resting positions, I begin to hear and see the collision's consequential carnage, water spewing and splashing as if from a decorative fountain in a pond. I hear off in the distance what sounds like glass. But it sounds too thick to be a window, too loud to be a drinking glass. It sounds like tiles in search of a resting place, probably from each of our kitchens, foyers, and laundry rooms.

As the dust begins settling, encouraged by time and the spraying of water, I start making out the extent of the damage to both homes. Where is the water coming from? The damage is not nearly as bad as I would have imagined. It *seems mostly cosmetic, at least from here, except, of course, the side where the two collided. The entire wall of both houses, where they met, couldn't possibly be fixed. Well, at least with the very little I know about home repair. Because her house is a two-story, I can make out the damaged interior of the exposed rooms on the second floor. Peering through my front window, I can see that the exterior wall also came down in my house as I can make out the interior of hers through it. Littering the front yards are countless pieces of evidence from the force of the massive collision. Pieces of wooden studs, chunks of concrete from both foundations, and walkway pavers are all over the place.*

I can now see that the water is coming from detached water supply lines from both houses. There are some sparks flying, accompanied by the buzzing and arcing of electricity. I can make out severed electrical wires convulsing uncontrollably near pooled water. Though not as bad as one might imagine, the damage between the homes is extensive.

As things begin settling, Anthoniel says, "Tim, tell me. What is it that you see?"

As I look around reticently, I respond, "I see massive destruction from her house colliding into mine."

"What you need to understand is that what you have witnessed is only from your perspective. From her perspective your house collided with hers. The reality of the situation is that both houses collided into one another. This is what takes place when two people get married." He explains with great patience and what seems like empathy.

"After marriage, there is much work the two of you will need to do.

- *Remove the walls and fix the damage in your home.*
- *Assist her with her home, though you cannot demolish or build anything.*
- *Together the two of you must rebuild the exposed area where the collision took place.*
- *Together the two of you must build a completely new structure to surround your individual homes. You must become one before Jesus and the rest of the world.*
- *Together the two of you must maintain the entire structure."*

"These are your assignments. The day you marry you must begin immediately. Exposure to the world for a prolonged period will leave your marriage susceptible to outside influences and it will come in all forms, from both the obvious and the least likely of places. These outside sources are drawn to exposed areas like honeybees to a flower. You must protect your home! You must

become one. Remember: the Holy Spirit will help you. I will be here, but my involvement is limited. Your wife will also be your helper."

"I don't understand. How long will all of this take? It looks pretty bad."

"This will be a lifelong process but do not be discouraged. Take heart—it is a process that should be enjoyed. Together the two of you will build lasting memories. Again, you will have help all along the way. Both of you must maintain this marriage as it will be under constant attack from the enemy without and from the enemy within."

"The enemy within?" I asked, shrugging my shoulders, arms bent toward him at the elbows, palms up, feeling childlike, much like a child's response when you ask something he or she doesn't understand.

"Yes—your old memories of you and the things you did, and her old memories of her and the things she did. Your individual desires will fight against what you are destined to become. For now, you must understand . . . becoming one does not require one person to surrender who he or she is to become what the other person is. Becoming one requires that each of you bring your strengths and your weaknesses to the table. Together you must negotiate through your coexistence. What will you do when both of you have lack in an area of great concern? The synchronicity between the two of you must be choreographed. The task is challenging.

"Hey!" he barks, taking me completely off guard. "All of heaven celebrates with you." He gives me an encouraging, side-fisted, gentle punch to the shoulder.

I thought only, "Yeah, no pressure there."

"Now go. I will see you soon."

Everything begins to fade.

The individual homes have collided.
Extensive and moderate damage is visible.

As it was in the beginning with Adam, each of us is given responsibility for tending to our own "Eden." Whether our Eden sits on square footage or on acres, has no children or sixteen, is supported by the help of a social service, or there's billions of dollars in income, the assignment set before every married man is exactly the same. Gentlemen, the assignment is the same regardless of socioeconomic status. Single and planning to marry, newlywed or decades in, and divorcé are all given the same test and rules of order. Being of a certain race or your family name does not provide anyone with an advantage. Finally there is a level playing field for all the players, but there is no competition! We can help one another over the finish line, and we are expected to do so.

I believe reading this book demonstrates wisdom and foresight as it contains valuable information to help prepare the hearts and minds of the man of God for marriage. As with Adam, we are given the things to do along with things not to do. In them we will find life and death. Will we choose life or follow after Adam believing life is too restrictive, consequently choosing death? Unlike Adam, we already have a pretty good idea of the consequential gravity of the choices set before us.

Marriage is that unique place where husband and wife work best together for getting across the finish line. Our physical conditioning is entirely irrelevant in this race. However, our spiritual conditioning is vital.

QUALIFICATIONS FOR THE POSITION OF A GODLY HUSBAND. Although the qualifications listed below are not actual ones for a godly husband, it seems quite reasonable that they could be used by us as a guide for holding the title. I acknowledge up front that there is an unmistakable difference between running a home and operating a church as an overseer, deacon, or elder for whom these requirements are written. In Paul's first letter to Timothy, he explains the qualifications for overseers:

> Here is a trustworthy saying: Whoever aspires to be an overseer desires a noble task. Now the overseer is to be above reproach, *faithful to his wife*, temperate, self–controlled, respectable, hospitable, able to teach, not given to drunkenness, not violent but gentle, not

quarrelsome, not a lover of money. *He must manage his own family well* and see that his children obey him, and he must do so in a manner worthy of full respect. (If anyone does not know how to manage his own family, how can he take care of God's church?) He must not be a recent convert, or he may become conceited and fall under the same judgment as the devil. He must also have a good reputation with outsiders, so that he will not fall into disgrace and into the devil's trap. (1 Timothy 3:1–7 NIV, emphasis added)

And for deacons, he outlines the following:

In the same way, deacons are to be worthy of respect, sincere, not indulging in much wine, and not pursuing dishonest gain. They must keep hold of the deep truths of the faith with a clear conscience. They must first be tested; and then if there is nothing against them, let them serve as deacons. ...A deacon *must be faithful to his wife and must manage his children and his household well.* Those who have served well gain an excellent standing and great assurance in their faith in Christ Jesus. (1 Timothy 3:8–10, 11–13 NIV, emphasis added)

Paul writes a letter to Titus outlining the requirements for elders:

An elder must be blameless, *faithful to his wife*, a man whose children believe and are not open to the charge of being wild and disobedient. Since an overseer manages God's household, he must be blameless—not overbearing, not quick–tempered, not given to drunkenness, not violent, not pursuing dishonest gain. Rather, he must be hospitable, one who loves what is good, who is self–controlled, upright, holy and disciplined. He must hold firmly to the trustworthy message as it has been taught, so that he can encourage others by sound doctrine and refute those who oppose it. (Titus 1:6–9 NIV, emphasis added)

Clearly, some cannot be requirements for getting married. "Faithful to his wife," "must manage his own family well and see that his children obey him," come *after* being married and having children. We should see these as things we need to learn through on–the–job training.

Although not written, I feel that in the very same way Paul qualifies an overseer, deacon, and elder, the remaining traits can qualify husbands and fathers. Regardless of our past and even our present, it all begins with us, and it must begin today. It starts in our own homes. Let God be God. Let our wives be the women they are called to be. All we have to do is be the men God calls us to be! Together we can be the standard God raises up as a hedge against the flood of the enemy's deception and evil in the world around us.

Proverbs 18:22, which reads, "He who finds a wife finds a good thing," seems to be the perfect opener for the married men section. What thoughts jump into your mind after having read it? Did you laugh hysterically? Did you scoff? Or did you say, "I know that's right"? Depending on how long we've been married, it is likely that most of us have thought something similar at some point. By "most of us" I mean our wives too. No sir, you are not the only one with a similar array of thoughts and feelings. In fact, every time she picks up your dirty socks from off the floor or asks you to use a cup holder for the "gazillionth" time, she may ask, "What in the world did I get myself into?"

One bit of irony about marriage is that single people tend to want to be married while married people often complain about it, telling single folks to appreciate where they are. What a dichotomy! The reality of the situation is that for the most part, married people do see marriage as being a good thing. However, our experiences with its goodness may not come around as often or stick around as long as we would like. You don't need to hear these words from a doctor of anything—marriage is not always easy. Neither is marriage always fun. Throughout marriage there are mountaintop moments as well as valley moments.

Here's a question for you: Have you ever been in the valley so long that you started dissecting Proverbs 18:22 and while doing so, got yourself hung up on just the first five words? Is it just me and my network or have you ever said to yourself, I am married but there is no way I would call this 'a good thing'? You do remember that God does not lie, right? Yet that is not how our experience might lead us to describe it. How does one resolve the discrepancy between God's truth and present (or previous) reality? The thoughts start rolling around in the brain. Here comes our attempt to close the disparity between what we know to be true and what we are experiencing.

Well, it does say "finds a wife." Is it possible that I found a woman and not a wife? Maybe she is not wife material and that is why this marriage is not a good thing. God didn't say he who finds a woman finds a good thing, though logic dictates that it takes a woman to make a wife. How about this one? If she sought me out across a crowded room, doesn't that really mean *she* found *me*? No wonder it's not working! Maybe we start pointing at the Bible itself. This book was written in a bygone era, when things were very different, apparently much easier to live in than it is today. Or perhaps God did not mean that for me, but if he did, *she* sure is messing this up! A lot of Christians blame the devil for putting thoughts like those in our minds. But let's just face it—those thoughts are our own best attempt to make sense of our situation as we see it in that moment.

If you are married and you've never had thoughts like those, then you know by way of personal experience that God and King Solomon (whom God spoke with and granted unprecedented wisdom and knowledge) are spot on. May he continue to bless you that you may never have those thoughts. If you are single and reading this, in no way are those comments meant to dissuade you from getting married. After all, this book is all about getting the most out of marriage by way of God's blueprint.

What God says about marriage is not isolated to certain people. He is not partial. Finding a wife and a good thing is not wishful thinking. It is truth and it is available to every God-fearing married man. Timothy affirms for us that all Scripture is inspired by God (2 Timothy 3:16). That means that in this case, God gave inspiration to Moses and Solomon, to give to all his people thereafter. Marriage is a good thing!

Are you thinking, *Easier said than done*? I agree. It is much easier to say what we should do than it is to do what we've said. Only with God does saying and doing require the same level of effort. Walking with God is a faith walk. We need to be able to view the world in two ways: what we see/live and what God says. One is in the flesh the other is in the spirit, respectively.

Here's something for mental imagery. Not too long ago I purchased my first pair of bifocals. Because I was experiencing bouts with vanity, yes, I forked over extra cash to get the bifocal lenses without their telltale signs—the lines. If you don't know anything about bifocals (God bless ya!) I need to explain them as it is important for the metaphor I will use shortly. Each bifocal lens is divided. The top part has the wearer's usual prescription. The bottom part uses magnification and is exclusively for reading things that are close (such as books, computer screens, menus, and such). As you might imagine, using bifocals requires up and down movement of the head and/or glasses for different uses.

True followers of Christ are given a pair of spiritual bifocals. The top allows us to see the natural world (present condition). The bottom half of the lens sees the natural world, but it is magnified by faith. Some people have strong faith (magnification) while others' magnification is weaker. In this case, unlike with regular glasses, we want strong magnification. It is through this part of the lens that we are able to see what God says. To see that, as you may have already guessed, means that we must tilt our heads upward (a positive disposition with expectancy). As it is with earthly bifocals, we should not look out of either half exclusively. Too much tilting up and you lose grip of reality. It is impossible to please him if we look through only the top half. With these glasses a married man can see present reality, discord between him and his wife. But through faith he can have confidence that he has favor with him and that everything he sets out to do will prosper.

Let's now get back to the actual verse and break it down. "He who finds a wife finds a good thing" presents us, minimally, with two ways of reading this verse, and both seem to be good options. Is the "good thing" finding a wife or is it marriage? Is there a legitimate reason for two perspectives? After all, it is not possible to be married without a wife.

The word *thing* has a positive and negative connotation based on its context. We are going to talk only about its "positive" use. Back in 1982 Michael Jackson recorded a song called "P. Y. T." ("Pretty Young Thing"). I just did the math on the release date in my head, now thinking, *Whoa! I'm getting old!* Based on the lyrics (and video), we know with confidence that *thing* is not derogatory. It was not sung with malice or the intention of objectifying women. In other words, a woman being referred to as a "pretty young thing" was a compliment. Part of my audience knows this. However, there is another part who is completely in the dark and never looked at *thing* as a reference to a woman.

One perspective is that in Proverbs 18:22 King Solomon used *thing* to refer to a woman (as M. J. did). In full context, it may very well be that Solomon was saying he who finds a wife finds a good woman (or lady or female). After all, what is the find in its initial use? It's a wife. But is that necessarily true? Maybe. Nevertheless, if that is how you remind yourself that the woman you love is a good woman, continue as you were. I see this perspective extremely helpful when a marriage is in one of those "valley moments." The fact of the matter is that you are looking at her in a positive light, through what I would refer to as your corrective lens—faith—while reality catches up. Nothing wrong with that!

Now the other perspective, "the good thing" is referring to marriage itself. I can see that equally well, reminding me of Rubin's vase. Err . . . umm . . . or is it Rubin's two faces? In Rubin's image it is possible to see either one vase or two faces. Both would be correct. Is it that God intends for both of them to be true? Surely there are some scholars who want to get into sentence structure and all the parts of speech. Yeah, I'll admit that I have no such inclination. Regardless of the semantics, I believe either perspective can be useful, and I believe neither perspective is harmful.

Flip back with me to Genesis 1:31—"God saw all that He had made, and behold, it was very good. And there was evening and there was morning, the sixth day" (NASB). What was very good? All that he made! Wait—I should be more detailed here. All that he made before man and woman was "good." It was only *after* creating man and woman and giving them dominion over everything did he look at it all, calling everything "*very* good." Was "very good" limited only to a wife or to marriage? It seems absurd to think one or the other when viewed from that perspective.

Could Solomon have said that he who finds a wife (gets married) finds a very good thing? I believe that he could have. So far, being married is a "situation" that could be described as being both good (Solomon) and very good (God). I believe that marriage as God sees it is something that neither man nor woman can affect. In other words, marriage stands all by itself as being a good thing. If that is not convincing enough, let me try again by way of example.

Everyone probably agrees that the Internet has both its benefits and drawbacks. The Internet makes it possible for anyone to fix almost anything by watching how-to videos on YouTube. Almost anyone can now take remote courses at colleges, universities, and various training facilities worldwide on nearly every subject. Pop-pops can talk to their grands, high school friends can reconnect after forty years, and famous people can speak directly with their fans anywhere around the world almost instantaneously.

At the same time there is a much darker side that also exists along with the Internet's benefits. The Internet makes it possible for people to remotely connect to other computers to steal sensitive information. I know. I get letters warning me that my data has been compromised at least quarterly. Someone *has* to do something about this. I digress… my apologies. Hospitals can be locked out of all of their patient records until a large ransom is paid. No longer are bullies contained to the classroom—they are all over the world looking for people of all ages to virtually assail. And those only graze the surface! Remove every file from every connected computer. Remove all the folks behind the connected computers, and there we have it, an incredibly wonderful and powerful tool with enormous positive potential. We have just traveled back in time to the sixties, a time when the Internet was little more than a concept written on a chalkboard in some lab underground (presumably). The Internet at that moment in time most people would probably agree was a good thing.

Jumping back to today, files and folks present, the Internet is good, although it is now used outside of its original purpose and design. Here's the thing: As in the case with the Internet, it is the case with marriage. It is our (man and woman's) fallen state that leaves marriage susceptible to the mess we can sometimes find ourselves in, and like the Internet, it is because marriage is operating outside of its purpose and design.

Nevertheless, despite all of that, it seems reasonable to conclude that God reminds us through Solomon that marriage is good. Here is more good news: marriage is good with man and woman *included,* that is, despite our fallen condition. In short, we have the potential to experience the good God sees in marriage, but we need to know what God says about it and walk within his precepts in order to experience all of its goodness.

So what is it that God expects from us as husbands? We will endeavor to answer that in great detail in part four of this book, "Commands and Exhortations." I will begin each topic with an ordinance-based Bible verse for us men. As a courtesy heads-up, some of the verses are not included in their entirety. I did this for the sole purpose of focusing our attention on only what God expects of us as husbands. We are not concerned with the expectations that God has placed on wives because those expectations fall squarely on their shoulders. Husbands are not held accountable for what God expects of wives *unless* husbands are keeping wives from walking out God's will for their lives as marriage partners. If we are doing that, there is no way we are walking out his plan for us. Husbands are responsible for all of their God-given responsibilities *regardless* of what the wives do (or do not do). The Bible teaches that at the day of reckoning every one of us will have to give an account for our actions and inactions (Matthew 12:36; Romans 14:10–12; 2 Corinthians 5:9–10). Personally, I believe it's doubtful that any husband will be able to stand before the Holy One and be excused were he to say, "Well, I would have done what you told me to do, but what happened was that my wife . . ." Let me ask a rhetorical question: How well did that work for Adam? I am confident that no man after Adam will get very far with that excuse either.

With the wife's responsibilities in mind, I am still standing at the fork in the road. To the right, leave out her God-given responsibilities. Veering off to the left, include her God-given responsibilities. Why the conflict? Maybe it's just me, as I know my former track record, but I do not want to be an accomplice in any finger-pointing or excuse-making. Including her responsibility makes it too easy to say, "Well, she isn't doing this, so I couldn't do that." Doing so will not help our case, and I feel like the impact this book *should* have for men and marriage will effectively be diminished. On the other hand, I completely understand that marriage does not happen in a vacuum. I am still waiting to see where the Spirit leads.

Over my many years of married life, I have searched the Bible looking for anything and everything that would help me in this endeavor. I have researched the Scriptures and found ten precepts set before us as married men by God. There are a few others, but I included only one whenever two or more were essentially the same. The order in which they appear is not based on importance but their location in the Bible, hopefully making it easier for you to navigate through yours.

DIVORCED MEN

What a beautiful day it is today! Whenever I am out in the yard, I get lost in the creative splendor of our amazing God. He created all of this for me. How others do not see Him I cannot understand. Of course, you never really contemplate as much as a child but as adults . . .

The sun is shining. Scattered across the vastness of the deep blue sky are bright, puffy clouds of all shapes and sizes. Birds of all types, male and female, talking to one another, but to me, all I hear are chirps, caws, tweets, and whistles. I can hear movement off in the distant brush and the telltale signs of some four-legged animal out making its rounds. I'm guessing it's probably a rabbit—they are all over the place these days. Man, this hammock is one of the best things I bought since moving into this house. It's so peaceful . . . if life were only this peaceful.

I can feel shifting taking place from the inside. I am moving between serenity to angst, remorse, regret, and around again. After having been married for what seems like forever, I have come to realize that there is no equivalent place like self-actualization in marriage. There is no such thing as home base, as there is in baseball, where the other team cannot touch you. There is no free space as there is in bingo. My marriage is all but shot. Where did it go wrong? Were there signs? It just doesn't matter anymore. It is what it is.

"Come!" calls the familiar voice. That is the last thing I remember before being pulled into the presence of the angelic being I have been talking with over the years, Anthoniel. This time he's different. His demeanor—I cannot put my finger on. Anger? Disappointment? Nevertheless, I bow in respect.

Upon rising and opening my eyes, no longer is there nothingness, but all of life appears to exist around one massive house. I'll never get used to this mode of transportation. Birds. Sun. Trees. But no other people, cars, or houses. It reminds me of a post-apocalyptic scene in a movie prior to the earth being overrun by plant life. The one big house in front of me has sustained extensive damage. Siding is falling off in different places. Mortar in its decorative stone facia needs to be repointed. Some of the pickets in the fence are missing, others crooked, with some standing as they should. The mailbox is open, stuffed beyond its capacity, and its entire post is leaning. The windows are dirty. A couple of them are broken. It is hard to tell if this house is lived in. As far as I can see, it does not appear to be.

"Do you know what you're looking at?" Anthoniel asks.

"Uhhh . . . an abandoned house, but that is too obvious to be the correct answer to your question."

"Well, you are right about the latter, but that house is not abandoned. You, your wife, and your kids live here."

Staring with what has to be a look of shock, disappointment, and confusion, I respond, "Someone lives here? We live here? What happened?"

"You have not done what I asked you to do the last time we spoke. I told you—together the two of you must rebuild the exposed area where the collision took place. Together the two of you must become one and maintain your marriage."

In great shame I ask, "This is our doing?"

"No. This is because of what you did and what you did not do. This is about your failure to do as you have been directed," he notes with fierceness. "You started out fine but by the sixth year providing for your family became your priority. You spent more time chasing position and prosperity, neglecting what was most important. You forgot—I AM is your provider."

He continued: "You spent more time in your separate homes building yet more walls and reinforcing the old ones. But this is not yet complete. You are looking at what is. Now you will see what will soon take place."

Suddenly I hear an indescribable roar. I have no choice but to ball up tightly, wincing and covering my ears. But I am watching all that is taking place. It looks as if it starts from the rear roofline. Along a near perfect seam it begins. The roof shingles start tearing and flying away along the middle, exposing roof wrap and plywood. I hear what sounds like tearing, and I see the plywood splintering, cracking, ripping apart. Now roofing joists, insulation, creeping toward the front top corner of the house, siding, rigid insulation, house wrap, plywood—it is all tearing apart exposing studs, insulation, and drywall. The tear, all the way to the ground, and now the ground is rumbling and tearing open—it's an earthquake. The whole time I am witnessing this there is an intense feeling of a splitting sensation throughout my body. The pain is excruciating. The noise is debilitating.

The outside structure tears away and is taken into the air as if being pulled by what looks like a funnel cloud. The conjoined houses we started in six years ago are now visible. But they look terrible.

"What just happened?" I ask, not being able to take my eyes off what's in front of me.

"Wait. Watch." he orders.

The roar starts again. There is a huge gaping hole where the two houses meet above the roofline of my house. The separation begins there. It is as if two giant hands are reaching into that space. It looks like a pulling-apart as debris from the houses is tossed everywhere. The noise is unbearable. The separating continues. This needs to end. Suddenly it is over. Silence. Dust. House guts strewn everywhere.

"It is finished. Because you did not listen to all that I have said, this is your coming separation and subsequent divorce. At its worst, this did not have to be the result. He offered you his help too many times to count. You are too stubborn."

The carnage is mind blowing. My eyes are welling with tears, my nose stinging. As the tears begin their descent, I look around. I see her on the other side of the quake, standing in front of her house—my wife. We lock tear-filled eyes. Wiping her face, she turns. Then suddenly she is gone.

I am back in my hammock . . . awake and devastated.

Although not present, I hear Anthoniel's departing words: "He will ask you about this."

The outer home has been destroyed.
The individual homes have been torn apart.

The other day while driving down I-90, I noticed a billboard off to the side. Appreciating its creativity, I burst out into laughter.

"Did you see that billboard?" I asked my wife.

"No, I missed it. What did it say?" she responded while turning back and realizing it could not be read from behind.

It was an advertisement by a local law office. It read, "Honeymoon over?" with two busted couple's wedding rings. But after only a quick moment, its reality set in. That billboard was not funny. There is at least one part of one couple who is going through some really difficult times, difficult enough that he or she will make that call. It pained me to the core. Then I began thinking of all the other couples out there who are in that very same space. I felt horrible inside. You see, society makes separation and divorce seem so easy. It is far from that, and I am not talking about finances or kids or healthcare coverage. I am talking about the pain that comes from the two people separating that once had ironclad love for each other, a love that was once thought to be an enduring love. Separation is painful, but this comes only from the perspective that it was not a result of one or more forms of domestic abuse, although I would imagine in that case, separation does provide relief on some level, but probably will still result in some emotional pain for both.

No one talks about the emotional tearing, referring to the metaphorical home. No one speaks of the damage of separation, the wake of destruction. What happens to the walls the two of you took down together and their associated joy? Will those walls go back up?

What about the new walls you didn't realize you built as a consequence of the marriage? No one talks about those really. I guess in some way it could be what people refer to as "baggage." But see—here's the thing with baggage. It sounds as if we have the option to take it or leave it, as if we can lighten the burden by pulling it around on its wheels instead of carrying it. It doesn't really give us a true picture of what results from traumatic interpersonal experiences—walled rooms in our psyche. If you are in this place now, know that my heart goes out to you.

Regardless of how you slice it, divorce is outside the will of God. Here are the words directly from Jesus. We know all his actions and speech came from the Father. "Moses, because of the hardness of your hearts, permitted you to divorce your wives, but from the beginning it was not so" (Matthew 19:8 NKJV). Stressing a point here, it was Moses's edict that permitted divorce. Why? Because of the stubbornness of the people. God did not create marriage with a built-in divorce clause. Likewise, it is out of our own stubbornness that we divorce today. If both the husband and the wife would love each other as God commanded, there wouldn't be divorce. I know—people are people. Again, reminding you, I am not casting stones. I would have to set my stone down and walk away. Truthfully, I wouldn't have been there in the first place to have picked up a stone. I am just trying to be that voice for someone out there who is at or near the edge. Divorce is far worse and impactful on more things and people than ever imagined.

If it were possible to put the work associated with walking out God's principles for marriage on one side of a scale, then on the other side, dealing with *all* of the aftermath of divorce, the latter would be considerably heavier. Divorce is quick and at the outset appears to be less work and more freeing. Simply put, divorce is about self, even when we say it is for the children. It is out of our stubbornness (hard-hearted, hard-headed, stiff-necked) that we divorce. Let me be clear, though. It is the stubbornness of *at least* one person that precipitates divorce. I am not suggesting the recipient of domestic abuse is stubborn or that he or she should stick around for more beating physically or otherwise. What I am saying is that stubbornness is coming from the other person. It is an absolute refusal to abide by God's statutes on anger, violence, and love (among other commands).

"So then, they are no longer two but one flesh. Therefore, what God has joined together, let not man separate" (Matthew 19:6). I believe marriage to be one of those aspects of binding and loosing that we are permitted to do here on this earth (Matthew 18:18) as Christ's followers. When two people get married, they establish a marriage covenant before God, a binding contract. God sees that and binds the two together in heaven and assigns his ordinances upon the husband and the wife (this is when his requirements of such a covenant go into effect). Some will likely disagree with me on this, and that is perfectly fine. Whether we agree on this doesn't really matter. We should, however, agree that marriage is a relationship that God establishes and has a keen interest in developing and protecting.

Over the years I have come to realize the gravity of this offense despite how relatively simple the divorce process is made to be. Speaking only for myself and those around me who have gone through this experience, the gravity of divorce is not realized until after the documents have been ratified. Make no mistake about it—divorce is like a self-perpetuating virus. Its desire is to affect and infect everyone who comes in contact with it. Divorce wants to remind you of its presence at every possible opportunity, preferably when you least expect it. It does not want to be forgotten.

I believe when most people recount the words of our Savior "Let not man separate," they are looking at them from an outside-in perspective, almost as if it is limited only to the person or persons outside the marriage (the adulteress/adulterer). The verses use *man,* as in *mankind.* Does that include family and friends who incite divorce through "encouraging words"? What about their respective attorneys? It's just a question to ponder, not a declaration. Either the husband alone or the wife (and in some situations both) are also responsible parties. It is not just the guy or girl a spouse got tangled up with. Does this verse imply some sort of curse on all those involved? That I cannot say, but it does sound as though it could be a warning, though it does not scream as loudly as "Woe to the man or woman who facilitates the dissolution of marriage wherever and whoever they may be."

This section was not written with the purpose of offending anyone who has gone through divorce or to those considering divorce. It is here to help us understand that our experiences, good and/or bad, leave indelible marks on us and others well into the future. If the divorce was due to a lack of trust in the marriage, that lack of trust will be coming right along for the next ride. Was it a lack of communication? Yes, that too is coming along for the next ride. How about abuse? Coming. The point is that all these things and more either created new walls or reinforced walls that never came down at some earlier time. More rooms, different rooms—all of these are part of us now. While getting into a new relationship may be far from a divorcé's immediate thoughts, interactions with others are almost inevitable. After all, it is this author's argument that we are created to be together.

In the time between relationships it is best to ask God to reveal all lingering issues, though we usually have a good idea of what they are. Ask him to reveal and heal. If you need to speak with someone, be sure he or she is capable of providing support from a biblical perspective.

WIDOWED MEN

From God's perspective, the widowed man has been released from his responsibility as husband (Romans 7:2–3). While the referenced verses speak of the widow, the "rule," I believe, applies to the widower in the same way.

While I am not pushing anyone to remarry, as in the rest of this book I am just providing biblical information that we might stay within the will of God. Timing, desire, and opportunity all play a major role in whether to seek the companionship of another woman. I wouldn't dare suggest "replacement." That said, God has purpose for you, and walking it out continues. As with the case of every other man, regardless of marital status, this biblical truth remains—it is not good for you to be alone. This does not mean that you cannot be alone or that you should not be alone—but that it is not good for you to be.

While I have no fictional account or graphic for this situation, I do not believe either is necessary. In my opinion, the widower seems to be a combination of all other marital statuses with his own uniqueness. Allow me to explain.

In some ways you are like the single man, free to decide, borrowing from Paul, "to remain in that state" or to marry. But you have an advantage over the single man in that you've garnered experience, knowledge, and hopefully wisdom from being a husband. It is because of this that you are also like the married man, having greater insight over the single guy. But there is still another similarity and that is with the divorcé. You have had your complement violently taken from you although the circumstances surrounding the separation are obviously different.

I suspect, as with the rest of us, that you've done some remodeling in your own home. You have most likely said or done things (good and bad) to cause your wife to have done some remodeling of her home when you were together. And just like every other man, you probably have walls that went up while being married. This is the time to work on self, removing walls that incumber godly relationships with others. Seek godly help if needed.

But this is where you are uniquely different. It is reasonable to feel like building a wall around your heart after experiencing such a profound loss. Who would *want* to go through that again? You could feel that no other woman deserves to be in that special place your wife possessed. Those are fair and reasonable thoughts and feelings. If you will allow me to respectfully share a truth with you, I would be most grateful. The truth is that your heart is not meant to be isolated from but to be shared with others. Now whether you decide to share it at its deepest level with another godly woman is a choice only you can make in your own time.

My recommendation to you is to continue growing, pressing toward the mark for the prize of the high calling of God. While we are on this earth, we will have encounters with others and God has expectations of us as disciples that glorify him before others. This time must not be used to "sow wild oats" because you are without obligation to another woman. Remember: we are all under God's command to flee from sexual immorality (fornication). As you continue maturing, you will be better prepared for another woman of God if so desired.

THE WOULDWORKER'S TOOLBELT

As men of God, we should already know about and wear at all times the full armor of God. It is worn to protect us because "our battle is not against flesh and blood, but against the rulers, against the authorities, against the world powers of this darkness, against the spiritual forces of evil in the heavens" (Ephesians 6:12 HCSB). The armor of God is largely for defensive purposes. For the more offensive strategies, I made up my own toolbelt. In it I keep the following tools: joy, peace, forbearance, kindness, goodness, faithfulness, gentleness, self-control, and love (see Galations 5:22–23). One of the coolest tools I have is love, because it's a lot like a multifunctional Swiss army knife. The love tool holds patience, kindness, honor, self-sacrifice, temperance, forgiveness, trust, hope, and perseverance. It also has protection against envy, boasting, and arrogance.

Unlike the tools we collect for our homes and jobs, love never breaks down or wears out (see 1 Corinthians 13:4–8). If you are asking yourself, "How do I get these tools?" I believe they are given to us by the Holy Spirit at the moment of indwelling. When we are walking "in" any of them, we are on the offense. Being patient with others is an offense strategy as it mitigates others from being defensive with us. However, these tools are also defensive. When someone for what seems no reason attacks our character, we respond with kindness. Just as with the whole armor of God, we need to carry these tools with us at all times. As we do, we get used to them. Carrying them around and using them becomes more natural. There is no need to look down to find the right tool to use—we find it without looking. No longer will it take focused effort to use.

While our marriage at this time might seem insurmountable, it is not. We have all the tools we need to be the best husbands we need to be. We must be sure always to use them. Here is one such example. One of the precepts we will discuss later in this book is about not treating our wives bitterly (part four— "Be Sweeter"). Those of us who use patience, kindness, love, honor, and temperance will have no problem with this command at all. For those of us who do have a problem, it is just a matter of using the tool so that it becomes like muscle memory or a passive alarm. Using it will be something that you do not have to consciously think about.

Before we talk about what the job entails, we need to talk about the tools we must always carry. Looking at the job that God assigned to us as men can seem insurmountable. I would agree with that statement if the man of God is not aware of the tools available to him. Working on our marriage is an "until death do us part" job. Despite anything we've heard from others or experienced in the past, it is a great job. It has all the benefits and perks, and the "pay" is unparalleled by any other job. Onto the God-given job requirements . . . we made it.

IV

COMMANDS AND EXHORTATIONS

Husband and wife are fixing their homes together.

A GREAT MYSTERY

Therefore a man shall leave his father and mother and
be joined to his wife, and they shall become one flesh.
—Genesis 2:24 NKJV

When I think back to the weeks and days leading up to my wedding day,
what really sticks out in my mind is the anticipation and nervousness
during that time. The closer the wedding day got, the more those
feelings intensified. Never before had I experienced them so strongly,

not by a long shot. Actually, I could make a strong argument that having a baby surpasses that, so let me make an adjustment. Apart from my wedding day *and* having a baby, no other event in my life brought about so much anticipation and nervousness. But this book is not about parenthood but being a godly husband to your bride.

Staying on topic, as the day drew closer, I thought a lot about marriage and what it means. Some thoughts were inspired by others' comments, some from television, but most from the observation of my parents. The one thing I don't remember ever contemplating was that we might become one flesh. Much less what God thinks!

Not a single person (Christian, worldly, married, divorced) had ever mentioned anything about my fiancé and I becoming one. Needless to say, my lack of information and wisdom on the subject led to a host of missteps and plenty of confusion. I needed to do something because I was making more of a mess than good memories. It wasn't long before I started reading the Word regularly and with the desire to get closer to God. That is when I realized that there are lots of things in it directed at husbands and wives. At the outset of my studies on the subject, I can honestly say that the phrase didn't make a lot of sense to me. I would like to share with you what my studies and of course the Holy Spirit has led me to understand as it pertains to the phrase "They shall become one flesh." Although we might have our own ideas or hear ideas from others, the biblical meaning is the one that *really* matters. It makes the most sense that we start with the creation of man and woman.

I really enjoy reading Moses's account of creation because for me I see his description of events as a very large, complex puzzle. We are not given all the pieces to the puzzle or a picture of marriage to look at as a key. The Bible provides most of the pieces while other pieces are made available through non-canonical works. Even with that information there are still many missing pieces. In my opinion, reading creation as if it were a normal story does not let the gravity of all that is taking place to sink in.

We are told all that God created and when (Genesis 2:1–17). It is up to this point that God had not yet created any living animals aside from man. Try forming a mental image of all that was taking place. Imagine vegetation in abundance (nothing overgrown and needing attending, green (or yellow, or red and vibrant), sun in the sky, peaceful and serene—probably a little eerie to us today as there would be no sound other than God speaking with man and the sound of footsteps on the grass in the cool of the day.

"Then the Lord God said, 'It is not good for the man to be alone; I will make him a helper suitable for him'" (Genesis 2:18 NASB). Wait! You mean to tell me that although God can do and has done everything for man just by speaking, that he was there to commune with him at any time or all the time—he saw that man had need for something else? It boggles my mind that God, being the source of all our needs, actually said man needed something else (not instead, definitely not more than) because it was not good for him to be alone. It was a need Adam himself didn't know he had. But God knew. Before sin was infused into subsequent generations, God said it was not good for Adam to be alone. That begs the question. If it was not good for man to be alone, why are single/divorced/unhappily married believers saying, "I don't need anyone else—all I need is God"? What is behind the mindset that we are somehow different from Adam? Are we more capable now than he was? There is considerably more mess that we face in this world now than, I believe, ever before. I believe the thought of not needing anyone else is sourced either by the ego, the enemy, or both.

Reverting to the verse, there is a two-word phrase we must dive into—"suitable helper." In this we get a very clear picture of what God intended for man. The word "suitable" in Hebrew is *neḡeḏ*, meaning "in front of" (part opposite; specifically, a counterpart, or mate). In Hebrew *ʿēzer* means "one who helps." Not much enlightenment there, right? At least at this point we know why man needed something—it was not good for him to be alone. All of creation thus far was unsuitable and was not the type of help God knew that man needed. God went back to his infinitely creative self in an effort to make something that was a suitable "counterpart."

> Out of the ground the Lord God formed every beast of the field and every bird of the sky, and brought them to the man to see what he would call them; and whatever the man called a living creature, that was its name. (Genesis 2:19 NASB)

For our purposes here, we will huddle around the beginning of the verse—"Out of the ground the Lord God formed every beast of the field and every bird of the sky." In context, we see that it is in direct response to verse 18. The beasts and the birds were created because God was "looking" for a suitable helper to resolve man's problem of being alone. We should be careful how we look at these events. First, God was not randomly trying to create things to see what would answer man's problem. That reminds me of my missing bolt dilemma. Most people complain of losing one sock—I can never find the right nut-and-bolt combination. Once in a while I run into a situation in which I need a nut and bolt for something. Without fail, the one size I need never has its matching bolt with it. So just as last month (and the month before and so on) I spend the next thirty minutes looking for its mate. Perhaps you know what I mean—the random trials scrounging around a junk drawer or tool box hoping to find the bolt. Too big. Five minutes and nine bolts later . . . too small. More digging . . . that's not it either. Off I go to the big-box store. *Again!* Without question God was not doing randomized trials like me!

Visualize it. Believe it or not, it helps. After all the creating and naming of creatures in search of a "suitable helper" for man, the answer to the problem remained elusive. But it was not a waste of time, as my bolt searching was. The entire process was purposeful in that God wanted *all* of his creation, Adam and those yet unborn, to understand that *nothing* else created as of this point was capable of standing next to man. The next verse, 20, solidifies this thought for us: "but for Adam there was not found a helper suitable for him" (NASB).

We should take this moment to dig a little deeper into the word *helper.* Perhaps we will find contextual application elsewhere in the Bible more helpful in our quest for understanding. Hopefully there is something beyond its definition as it does not provide us with any insight. When we look at how the word *ʿēzer* (translated as "helper") is used in just a few other places in the Bible, we gain its deeper, intended meaning.

- "The other was named Eliezer, for he said, *'The God of my father was my help,* and delivered me from the sword of Pharaoh'" (Exodus 18:4 NASB, emphasis added).

- "Blessed are you, Israel; Who is like you, a *people saved by the Lord, the shield of your help,* and He who is the sword of your majesty! So your enemies will cringe before you, and you will trample on their high places" (Deuteronomy 33:29 NASB, emphasis added).
- "Our soul waits *for the Lord; He is our help* and our shield" (Psalm 33:20 NASB, emphasis added).
- "My *help comes from the Lord,* who made heaven and earth" (Psalm 121:2 NASB, emphasis added).
- "It is your destruction, O Israel, that you are against *Me,* against *your help*" (Hosea 13:9 NASB emphasis added).

I added emphasis to each of these verses hoping to get this point across, that the same type of help God provides man is the *same help God knows man needs!* As a sidenote, it doesn't matter how I reword that sentence—its impact gets lost. I feel as disappointed as I do when trying to describe to someone what the Grand Canyon looks like or while I am showing someone a photo of me with the Grand Canyon as a backdrop. If you haven't been, its splendor and size just cannot be described in words. Nor can a photo or drawing convey that message. Every attempt is woefully inadequate.

Those verses provide an explanation for the type of "helper" God is seeking for man. He knows man should not be in this world alone, that is, alone in a world filled with lots of other things. While some may be scoffing at the idea that woman is that kind of help, there is one thing that I hope we can all come to agreement on. God *is not* man's assistant, underling, or one who plays second fiddle to man. Can we start there? If we can do that, I will build onto that in hopes we can come into full agreement on what woman really is to man.

To recap in brief, in all of creation up to this point not one suitable (opposite, or in counterpart to man) helper was found for man. So what does God do next that will create the perfect, opposite but equal helper?

> So the Lord God caused a deep sleep to fall upon the man, and he slept; then He took one of his ribs and closed up the flesh at that place. The Lord God

fashioned into a woman the rib which He had taken from the man, and brought her to the man. The man said, "This is now bone of my bones, And flesh of my flesh; She shall be called Woman, Because she was taken out of Man. (Genesis 2:21–23 NASB)

You likely already noticed this, but just in case I will go through it anyway. How did God create all of the previous "contenders"? Correct, from the dust of the ground. Where did man's suitable helper come from? She, woman, came from him! She was an extension of him. Spoiler alert! This is one reason we are to love woman as we love ourselves. It only makes sense. Woman is not a separate, lesser creation of the dust of the earth (well, by extension she is from the earth because man is) but created out of man. How is it possible to love self but not her (see Ephesians 5:28–29)? We will work through this later in the book.

Let's tease this out. Adam is entirely complete before Eve is created. A rib is removed from him and an entirely new creation – Eve – is brought forth. Adam is whole but no longer complete because part of him was removed to create Eve. He does not get that part back. Adam...watch this...is not complete without Eve's presence. On the other hand, Eve is whole but she was never complete to begin with. Why? Because she does not have all of what Adam had to begin with, only part. Just like Adams circumstance, Eve is not complete without Adam's presence. Man is not complete without woman and vice versa. Man and woman are but fractions of what they are together. This is why they must become one (husband and wife). Sound ridiculous? It isn't and it works the same, principally, as one man sinned and entered all of mankind (Romans 5:12–13). We, as descendants of Adam and Eve, inherited their likeness and nature. We need to keep this in mind as we work out God's commands for us as it pertains to marriage.

Imagine a very complex and beautiful mosaic. A completely intact piece of art made of individual pieces of colored gems, each gem complementing and contrasting one another in all the right places. When the sun hits them, only then are the intricate details and unmatched perfection truly observable. No angle is a bad angle, and no other light makes this possible. The value of this artwork is unknowable and unfathomable. Now cut out a section near the center. Neither the original work nor its removed piece is complete or the same. Although the artist has crafted another work from the removed section, the gems are not exactly complementing the added pieces as in the original piece. While whole, it is not complete. Even in the original work, though the extracted section is patched with new stones, they are not the same as what were removed. Somehow only when the two separate works are brought together do you see the masterful genius behind both. As the sun brings out the inflections in all the gems, it is only when *the Son* shines on man and woman (husband and wife) that their intricate details, unmatched perfection, can be observed. That little metaphor falls infinitely short in trying to compare it with what our creator did, but it is the best I can do, and I hope it is enough to help visualize what took place.

Previously, I mentioned God not being man's assistant, underling, or second fiddle. And if you did not already arrive at this conclusion, let me be very direct and say this: Neither is woman an assistant, underling, or second fiddle to man! Period. Full stop. I will say, though I should not need to, that I am not implying that woman is equal to God either. But we do need to be very careful in how we view our wives specifically and women generally (and by extension girls and young ladies). This goes hand in hand with another verse we will discuss later: 1 Peter 3:7. I have heard Christian men actually say that women are meant to be subordinate to men. Is that right? It is only when we view Genesis 1:26 through an arrogant lens that we arrive at that conclusion!

> Then God said, "Let Us make man in Our image, according to Our likeness; and let *them* rule over the fish of the sea and over the birds of the sky and over the cattle and over all the earth, and over every creeping thing that creeps on the earth." (Genesis 1:26 NASB, emphasis added)

When God said "Let Us make man in Our image," he was not speaking only of the male gender. Here is the proof—"*God created man in His own image, in the image of God He created him; male and female He created them.*" (emphasis mine). We can all agree that *man* does not always mean "male" but sometimes is used for "mankind" (that is, male and female). The Hebrew word *'āḏām* also means "mankind" (Strong 2001). Both were equal. Both were to have dominion. It was not until after eating the forbidden fruit that man's sinful nature of arrogance would kick in. In Genesis 3:16 God tells Eve (women) that because of her disobedience the following would result" "Your desire will be for your husband, And he will rule over you." I do not in any way believe this was God, borrowing a military term, busting Eve down in rank. Since then, men and culture followed this course as God prophesied to Eve thousands of years ago. Men of God, we do not have to fall into that faulty way of thinking. We have been given other instruction to follow (we will get there).

Today, as it pertains to the equality of women, is both what was *and* what was not intended. Women were created to rule—equally. Woman in God's eye is not inferior to man. But she was never intended to replace man or to stand on her own. Today the pendulum has swung to the other extreme. Same pay for the same work, yes. Same rights, yes. But she is not the same but a counterpart. How is counterpart defined? Merriam-Webster says—

A thing that fits another perfectly

1. something that completes: complement
   One remarkably similar to another
2. one having the same function or characteristics as another ("counterpart")

Hmm . . . I find that interesting! God sees the value in us together and has plans through us (husband and wife). It is the enemy that has deceived us from the truth for too long. He has told us that we do not need each other aside from the need to satisfy sexual urges and procreate. In the very same way men have blamed Eve for listening to the serpent, we have done and continue doing the same. Did God really say you are not to lord over her? (see Genesis 3:1) We have managed since that day to devalue the significance of what God has done between man and woman. Our actions are akin to those who unknowingly possess priceless heirlooms mistakenly selling them for a few bucks at a yard sale. I am not entirely convinced this is a mistake, though. Gross error, yes. Mistake, not so much. She is infinitely more valuable than we have been led to think and subsequently believe.

> For this reason a man shall leave his father and his mother, and be joined to his wife; and they shall become one flesh. (Genesis 2:24 NASB)

I feel compelled to poke the bear since I have a stick in my hand, and the bear is lying there asleep. Leaving Dad and Mom is an intentional and purposeful disconnection of a specific level of relationship we have with our parents. This disconnect must take place. But a disconnect does not mean we cannot or should not love, honor, or care for a parent (or parents). Neither does it mean we cannot or should not have close relationships with them. However, the reality of the situation is that our relationship with them cannot be as important or more important than the relationship we are to have with our wives. Parents should not impose their will in the marriage directly, through passive-aggressive means, manipulation, or other. If that situation exists for any of us now, we need to deal with it immediately but always in love and in honor of our parents (Exodus 20:12; Leviticus 19:3; Deuteronomy 5:16; Matthew 15:4; Matthew 19:19; Mark 7:10).

As with other commands in the new covenant, we can legitimately take this one step further. *Nothing* else comes before the missus. Any and everything else put before her is operating outside of the will of God regardless of how it is justified. It does not mean that nothing else is important but rather that nothing else is *as* important. We will discover more about this relationship as our study progresses. I will reiterate it, hoping that the message has a better chance of sinking in. *No* other single relationship is as important to God outside of him as the relationship between husband and wife. So why is it that we view it in such a cavalier way?

Unfortunately, intentionally or not, there are some things we allow to interrupt that hierarchy and by default the process of becoming one with our wives. In most cases, we allow careers, friends, family, hobbies, finance, and such to take her place in our hearts and minds. What makes it possible to make this misstep is that even our best intentions can camouflage life's purposeful distractions.

Generally speaking, men have considerable difficulty coping when we cannot provide for our families, but being a workaholic or overachiever has its own dangers. First and foremost, although things happen beyond our control, it takes us out of synch with God's order. I have personally made the mistake of putting things before my marriage. God is swift to warn us, and his alerts are progressive when unheeded. The very things we put before her he has no problem removing. My experience has been that he will give me a warning, a shot across the bow, if you will. The key is to recognize the warning as a warning as soon as possible. When I miss the cue, it always leads to another warning shot coming in a little closer. Let me give you an example. Many years ago I was one of those guys who loved their cars. I would keep them clean (even when they were beaters), I would pamper them, and I would boldly let my family know they were not allowed to eat in them. What happened next? Little things. Repairs, flat tires, and so on. But I failed to recognize what was really taking place. Guess what came next. An accident, and you know what? I still didn't see the message. When I got the car fixed or replaced, I continued worshiping my car-god, then another accident. And guess what? That's right—I still didn't learn. Another accident. Then I stepped back and took a good, hard look at my situation and considered what I was doing wrong. Nothing comes before my wife and nothing before my family. Since that revelation, I was in one "fender-scratcher" two decades later. That was not a lesson but a failure for the young lady to keep her eyes on the road instead of her phone. Here is my suggestion: take an honest look at your priorities. Are they in the right order? Have you been ignoring warnings? I plead with you to get your order right before God *helps* you get it right!

My prioritization issue was not malicious. I thought I was being a good steward. It was a problem that crept up on me and grew out of control. But some distractions are intentional. Sometimes we choose to make things priorities that should not be, thinking it is much easier to focus on other things than dealing with the problem we know needs our attention. We cannot ignore the possibility that the cause of the distractions can be something from the subconscious level, like a learned behavior we think is "normal." Self-centeredness by either spouse can lead to the formation of distractions. Sometimes being around other people make it very easy to get distracted. Always remember—others are not as concerned about your walk with God (our wives being part of that walk) as we must be. Sometimes the problem really isn't us but that of the enemy. The enemy takes pride in his work of killing, stealing, and destroying (John 10:10). He will do *anything* and use *anyone* to keep us from operating within the will of God, where the most power is. When we fall into his traps, it amounts to sin against God, consequently blocking our communing with him and its associated blessings. We must remain vigilant. As it is said these days, we need to keep our heads on a swivel.

When we operate outside of the will of God, all bets are off. But what tends to confuse the matter is that good things may continue happening. This often creates the appearance of God's blessing. Remember that good things happen to both the righteous and the wicked (Matthew 5:45). This is why we need to vigilantly check our walk against what the Bible says in *all* aspects of our lives (2 Corinthians 13:5). We must be careful when we know we are doing wrong somewhere not to think that success in some other area is God's approval. Or worse, that he is not aware of our disobedience. We could not be farther from the truth.

Back to Genesis 2:24 and leaving father and mother. In those few words we see that God is addressing all of us through Adam. In no way can this pertain to Adam and Eve, because they were first. Leaving parents *must* apply *only* to the rest of mankind. The message is quite clear that man is to leave Dad and Mom, be joined to his wife, that the husband and wife might then work together to become one flesh.

The NASB version uses "joined to his wife." However, the King James version uses "cleave unto his wife,: In this case, I prefer the KJV because the significance in the matter is made more emphatic. Here's what I mean by that. We might *join* other people when going out to eat. At checkout time we would *join* the end of a queue for the cashier to check us out. However, the word *cleave* connotes greater intensity. When it is cold inside, I will cleave to my blanket for warmth. Make no mistake about it—when I cleave to my blanket it is beyond what I do when I join others in the water at the beach. That, my friend, would at minimum be very uncomfortable. Worse case, worthy of arrest. In the inverse, when I sit and read in front of the television, my blanket doesn't join with me on the recliner. Here are other examples (adding my emphasis) with the use of the word cleave in the KJV of the Bible.

- "Thou shalt fear the Lord thy God; him shalt thou serve, *and to him shalt thou cleave,* and swear by his name." (Deuteronomy 10:20, emphasis added)
- "*Cleave unto the Lord your God,* as ye have done unto this day." (Joshua 23:8, emphasis added)

The very same cleaving that we must do with God is the *very* same cleaving we need to do with our wives. This really triggers a lot of questions in my mind; perhaps it does the same to you. I cannot help but wonder if there is any correlation between the relationship we have with God and the relationship we have with our wives. In other words, can I cleave to my wife but not to God? Can I cleave to God and not my wife? The first is idol worship. God is not going to let that continue uncorrected. The latter is flat-out disobedience, and that too God will deal with. In my opinion, the relationship we have with our wives is a type of relationship we are to have with our Savior. Maybe that is not yet clear to us at this point. My hope is that before the end, you will agree wholeheartedly with my claim. This is profound for those of us that are truly seeking God and his will for our lives above all else.

Staying with this a little longer because of its significance, *cleave to* or *joined to* is greater than the marriage tradition as we know it. We should *not* check *cleave/joined to* off our to-do list because we got married in some big church with 400 people or eloped to Las Vegas with two witnesses. Doing these things does not denote full compliance. I want to make this as plain but impactful as possible. If God expects us to cleave to our wives in the same way he expects us to cleave to him, cleaving *must* be more than just going through the pomp and circumstance surrounding marriage. I could provide many verses that prove this truth, but I will settle for just the following verses because they are hard hitting:

> Then the Lord said, "Because this people draw near with their words And honor Me with their lip service, But they remove their hearts far from Me, And their reverence for Me consists of tradition learned by rote, Therefore behold, I will once again deal marvelously with this people, wondrously marvelous; And the wisdom of their wise men will perish, And the discernment of their discerning men will be concealed. (Isaiah 29:13–14 NASB)

If you have not read the message in full context, I will let you know that the way God deals with Israel due to their lip service was not a desirable experience despite use of the expressions *marvelously* and *wondrously marvelous.* In my opinion only, the pomp and circumstance of a wedding, including its "Christian vows," can easily be nothing more than lip service. What meaning does any of that have with the husband-to-be and wife-to-be who aren't living for God? What meaning does it have with unbelievers who recite those vows?

To "become one flesh," as described in Genesis 2:24, has two different meanings. The first, being a much easier pill to swallow, is "to get married." But God sees marriage from a very different perspective (as the creator of it) than what it has become since he instituted it. We will learn through this text that marriage is significantly more complex. This book is about God's plan on how men are to conduct themselves through marriage. What marriage has become since is akin to using a book of matches to wedge under the leg of a lopsided table. Although the book of matches works to keep something from rolling off the tabletop, it is not at all what the manufacturer of those matches created it for. Some of us might personally know another couple who appear to be in the perfect marriage but do not know God. I do not wish to belittle those marriages as they do make for a wonderful life. But here is my question: If God measures its usefulness with different criteria than yours and mine (*His* criteria), what difference does it make what anyone but God thinks about it? That also includes the perspective of the husband and wife who are themselves in the "good marriage."

The second usage is the harder pill to swallow. Paul espouses (pun not intended) one that I have yet to hear anyone else ever talk about, and it is very important. Paul refers to becoming one as "a great mystery" (Ephesians 5:32). And no, Paul was not saying it was a great mystery because he was single and didn't understand why anyone would settle down with so many fish in the sea. It was not because he was thinking, *Why on Earth would any man go through this grueling punishment?* Not that it is either grueling or punishment.

We should recognize that *joined* is not a different way of saying *become one flesh*. Going back to English class from yesteryear when we learned about coordinating conjunctions, the word "and" is one of many coordinating conjunctions used for the purpose of connecting two or more clauses together. From its use and what we will learn from this text, we can infer that the process is multi-staged:

- leave dad and mom
- be joined to his wife
- become one flesh

This is a sequential event. You cannot jump past any one of the first two (or both) and go directly to three and be successful. We will also learn that *become* is not instantaneous. It is a process that takes place over time. How much time? Until death. How challenging that process is depends on the couple. We know that most couples, though married, never achieve oneness. This book's primary purpose is to bring to light God's essential requirements. I hope that knowing them will make the process a little easier so that the two can become one. When oneness is achieved, oneness must be maintained. It is not a finish line you cross but a daily duty/responsibility to be carried out. If you are asking, "What is involved with becoming one flesh?" unfortunately, this cannot be answered in one or a few sentences here. Instead, I will use the pages of this book to lay out the answer for us.

Back to our original broadcast. I believe some key information must have happened between Genesis 2:24 and the introduction of the serpent in chapter three. First, there must have been a fairly decent amount of time that passed. How much time we cannot know. Second, I believe that it is during that time that the two were probably in maintenance mode. Here is what we do know:

- God gave the instruction to Adam.
- Adam gave the instruction to Eve.
- Eve ate the forbidden fruit first.
- Adam followed.

Here is what we cannot know with certainty, but I believe:

- Adam did not eat the forbidden fruit because he was weak.
- Adam's disobedience was not consequential to Eve being a nag.

I believe Adam ate the fruit because the two were so much in tune with one another that they were like-minded and agreeable. I believe after Eve and Adam had a talk that he came into full agreement with what she said. If as some men argue, Eve was inferior in her thinking to Adam, wouldn't it necessitate that his following after her actually made him lesser of an intellect? I mean God spoke directly to him, but Eve convinced him to do it anyway. That doesn't take much of a stretch to realize—*if* that was the case.

The takeaway is not to be one flesh to the point of disobeying God's precepts but that husband and wife need to be one *while* being obedient to God's commands. In the book of Acts it is referred to as "one mind" or of "one accord." Becoming one does not mean losing oneself to another but the willful sacrifice of self, on both sides, in order that the two might become one. I hear lots of men say, "I'm looking for a strong, independent woman." I think, *Is that really what you want?* It seems to me that a woman wholly devoted to God above all else should be our desire. If she is in that place and you are in that place, I believe with all that I am that becoming one will be a cinch. There is a song that pops into my head from back in the day that is often played in ceremonious and joyous situations—"Ain't No Stopping Us Now" (by McFadden and Whitehead, released in 1979). In today's vernacular we might call this "a united front."

Marriage is one explanation for "becoming one flesh" but that is not enough to explain why Paul referred to it as a "great mystery" (Ephesians 5:32). Why call it that? Neither sex nor marriage are mysterious. In Paul's first letter to the church in Corinth he says something different and unexpected. "Do you not know that the one who joins himself to a prostitute is one body with her? For He says, 'THE TWO SHALL BECOME ONE FLESH'" (1 Corinthians 6:16 NASB). He draws a connection between becoming one flesh (Adam's statement) and having sex. Now that is truly a mystery! Is it really possible that from God's view sex is an agreement of a marriage commitment between man and woman? Is it phase one in becoming one flesh? Could that be why it is possible to remember former partners? After the two separate, is there something left behind with the other because of this connection Paul speaks of? Is sex more significant than we see it? With all these questions (and many more) bouncing around in my mind, it is now easier for me to relate to Paul's reference to this as being "a great mystery."

The following statement is not meant in any way to berate marriage. I have the utmost regard for marriage, of course, but here is a truth: Weddings that we attend seem to be little more than a ceremony, a "show," if you will, that allows others to be participative to varying degrees. After the kissing of the bride, jumping over the broom, smashing glasses, exchange of garlands, or lighting of candles, is it then that the relationship is made official in God's eyes? Thankfully this book is not an exposition on marriage, so further investigation into cultural differences isn't needed. What we should think about, though is this—with all of the cultural variations, is there a universal point in time when God says, "Because you have done [or said] this thing, I recognize the two of you as married"? Or does he make note of each culture and looks at the situation from our varying perspectives? With so many cross-cultural marriages taking place with the observation of both cultures in the same ceremony (or in two separate ones), which of the two is that point? Both? We can all agree that the two did not get married twice. I will walk to the edge of the plank by myself because what I am about to say is entirely in opposition with the world today. I doubt very highly that God cares anything about the pomp and circumstance surrounding marriage. The one thing that seems universal is the consummation of the marriage—the first act of sexual intercourse after all the pomp and circumstance. Is it possible that to God this act signifies marital commitment? While entirely unreasonable to most folks, I don't believe it to be a stretch to arrive at this conclusion.

Closing out this opening section—guys, we must realize that God has commanded that we become one with our wives. Becoming one is more than splitting all the bills down the middle. I'm convinced it is more than the marriage ceremony itself. It also seems to be the sexual act between the two. Becoming one is also a process that continues throughout the marriage. Trials, tests, and quite possibly temptation will come to validate our compliance. With that said, there may be some marriages that have been years in the making in which the two are walking in separate directions. How are we as husbands supposed to comply with God's command in those situations? It will not be easy, but it is possible to do all that you can to be compliant.

Pray and rely on God for help. We must get ourselves together if we are the reason oneness has not been achieved. If it is her, you cannot effectively change your wife's heart, right? I am not convinced that statement is entirely true. While it may seem like a lost cause, regardless of the reason, I don't believe it has to remain that way. If we could go back in time to the early days of our marriage and tell our wives that we are committed to becoming one as God commands, would she participate? I feel she would, and I feel she would have already been more than halfway there. But that begs the question—What happened (or did not happen) for her heart to change? *Something* happened over the course of time or perhaps more acutely that shifted her heart (thoughts and feelings) away from where it was to where it is now. Just as time changed her to where she is now, it will likely take time for her to change back. Marriages do recover. Even those that were counted out!

In my opinion, most men seem to be results driven. "Tell me what to do so I can do it." Unfortunately for a lot of life's situations, our expectation is that when we do it, its benefits should become evident as close to immediately as possible. I will not say *immediately* will never happen because God can do anything. However, I will say this—one of love's characteristics is longsuffering. Whether it is this situation or another, we must be patient and enduring and never quit doing the right thing despite ourselves.

I do not want to put all of that on the wife. Perhaps it is our hearts that changed. Maybe marriage has become nothing more than sharing bills, meals, and a bed. In this case, we need to get our hearts right. I am confident that none of us got on this boat with an apathetic disposition. We need to change our minds if for no other reason than to be obedient to the will of God. I believe that once the mind has shifted, our hearts will soon follow.

This looks like a good opportunity to address the elephant sitting in the room, a topic I am sure some of you are hoping I don't sidestep. I know this is going to create loads of consternation (putting it lightly) with many people, but this book was not written that I might make friends but deliver the truth. Could God have created another *man* for Adam? Absolutely not. Another man is neither an opposite nor a counterpart, but the *same*. I believe that is all that needs to be said on this subject.

Becoming one is more than getting married and having sex. It is a lifelong process that envelops the rest of our study in this section.

WITHHOLDING IS FOR TAXES

Nevertheless, because of sexual immorality, let each man have his own wife. ...Let the husband render to his wife the affection due her...And likewise the husband does not have authority over his own body, but the wife does.

—1 Corinthians 7:2–4 NKJV

You may have already realized that I removed those things Paul addresses to the wife from this section's topical verses. My doing so should not be interpreted as my believing that her part in all of this is not important. I do believe in fact that they are equally important. However, I am not yet convinced that including her responsibilities in any of this is necessary for this discourse. By the end of this book, after prayer and deliberation, together we will find out which direction I felt led to go in. Until then, this is about our being obedient to the will of God as it pertains to us as husbands.

On the surface, these verses seem rather straightforward, give your wife the affection she needs. However, I hope you will see by the end of this section that there is a bit more involved. When you first read the opening verses, whenever that may have been, did you think Paul was using affection only as an age-approved "church word" for sex? The NKJV uses the word affection (or conjugal duty). What comes to mind for you when you think conjugal duty? Because I have watched many prison-related movies and shows, I had the picture of a wife visiting her prison-bound husband for sex. I should have figured my understanding of the word was skewed; it came from TV. While I thought it meant blowing off "sexual steam," after further research on the subject, I began understanding that there's more to it. In case I am not the only one with the wrong definition, conjugal duty is not limited to sex. It includes every level of intimacy that takes place between husband and wife up to and including sex.

As men, we know that there are many things that can impact our ability to have sex, like age, health, physical shape, and so on. But affection is much broader than having sex. What about the other duties that fall under the general term affection? We must remember that neglecting those over time can be detrimental to marriage. Most likely Paul is not talking about those reasons for not having sex but two others that are a bit more self-centered: a lack of interest and outright withholding. Regardless of which it is, it is clearly a problem and, as Paul warns, can lead to sexual immorality. Paul begins this subject with "because of infidelity" and then goes into the means by which we are to avoid it. If there weren't an issue with sexual immorality there would be no need to write what he is about to write. Please keep in mind that

Paul is writing a letter to a church with regard to its members, not the world outside.

We need to fully understand that sexual immorality is significant in the eyes of God, so much so that he will step in to help prevent it. He refers to his stepping in as "make the way of escape" (see 1 Corinthians 10:13). Numerous Scriptures warn us of the severity of this issue, too many to include them all here. But what complicates the study is that sexual immorality is referenced in different ways between Bible translations as well as within the same translation. We would find the following synonymous references: fornication, adultery, immorality, unchastity, wickedness, gross immorality, acts of immorality, and more. Nevertheless, the point again is that this sin (however referenced) is significant in the eyes of God. Please read Malachi 3:5; Acts 15:20; Romans 1:28–32; 1 Corinthians 5:1; 1 Corinthians 6:9; 1 Corinthians 6:18; 1 Thessalonians 4:3; and James 4:4, for example.

There is a subtle yet significant difference between lack of interest and withholding, and we will talk about them in this section. Although they can lead to the same sexual sin, I chose to address them separately because it is too easy for a man on the one side to finger-wag the man on the other side (see Luke 18:11). Brothers, we need to understand that those are two different sides of the same coin! Both acts have the potential to lead to the same sin, having the same consequences. We should take care to steer clear of both offenses. We should come to the realization that we must stop, not look for someone else to blame but own it and fix it ourselves.

Do men really lose interest in sex? Yes, it can happen for legitimate reasons, including naturally as we age or from health problems. I believe we can set those aside and talk about the things that can result in dissatisfaction potentially leading to a loss of interest altogether. When left unaddressed, these among others can lead to immorality on either side.

- not happy with how often it happens
- it rarely looks the way it does on TV
- boredom due to a lack of spontaneity

- always needing to be the initiator
- the wife being too demanding: "Do it this way!" or "Not that way!"

Now compare those reasons above to withholding where sex is used to communicate, hurt, force change, and/or coerce, manipulate, and control. (Smith 2023) Regardless of which is the case, both can lead to sexual immorality. It is the fact that sexual immorality openly exists in the church and no one is doing anything about it that upsets Paul. Did you catch that? Sexual immorality is knowingly taking place *within* the church, but no one is coming against it! Hmm—doesn't seem that things have changed all that much after all this time.

I am perfectly fine with admitting I am no expert on withholding or losing interest, but I do believe distraction is missing or could perhaps be its own category. If the enemy can use others to distract husband or wife, he will. For the believer, self-sacrifice and stewardship are important tenants of the faith. The enemy uses guilt and compulsion to distract and disempower a God-fearing marriage. That seems to get lost. I will use a word that we are sensitive to. The enemy uses guilt and compulsion to emasculate marriages. Distractions can lead to disinterest, which can lead to sin. The sin can happen from either the husband, the wife, or both. Here is an example: The husband is actively visiting the sick and shut-in, going to funerals of family members in the congregation, and tries to attend graduations and birthday parties as part of his role in the church. Some of these are beyond the interest/responsibility of the wife as a lay member of the church. His dedication leaves her feeling neglected and vulnerable. Joe Shmo (I believe that's how he spells his name) from the usher board runs into her quite often, and consequently an "innocent" friendship develops. Innocent friendship turns into regular conversation. Now the husband's sin — putting everyone else before his wife develops into a loss of intimacy (without malice) that she needs and has a right to. She consequently raises the stakes in her friendship with Joe and begins and intimate relationship with him. This all began without malice, by forming an unhealthy relationship with another man because her needs weren't being met by her husband. That leads to adultery, now prejudicial to the marriage. Usher Joe is not off the hook, of course, for he has also committed sin (we know this as everyone blames Joe). We will go into this further later, but there are potential implications for other related parties to suffer as a result of this adulterous relationship! I know—what a mess!

Hopefully this fictitious example keeps you aware of the vulnerabilities we are all susceptible to in our marriages. Let me make sure I am clear about this. Men, the lack of interest and diminished sex drive is breeding ground for sin. Do you remember God's conversation with Cain? In Genesis 4 Cain is upset with Abel because God accepted his offering while Cain's was not. God says, "If you do not do what is right, *sin is crouching at your door*; it desires to have you, but you must rule over it" (Genesis 4:7 NIV, emphasis added).

Imagine, in either case, an evil demonic creature named "Adultery" sitting in the corner of your home peering through its empty, dark eyes, its fangs extending outside its upper lip, saliva dripping. It is rubbing its hands together menacingly. One can only imagine its thoughts. Maybe it's not in your home because neither of you are there. Maybe it is riding in the car with you or your wife, sitting in an office chair in either of your offices. Or perhaps it and its menacing friend are covering both of you, waiting for the perfect time to make a move. Just typing this presents a scary and disheartening feeling, yet I am only making it up. I imagine it's actually much worse than that, a story that only Clive Barker, John Carpenter, or Wes Craven could best deliver.

With regard to withholding, as I studied more on the topic, it occurred to me rather quickly that, unbeknownst to me, I was guilty of gender bias. Before doing research for this book, I thought only women withheld sex to manipulate and punish their husbands. As truth would have it, there are some men who withhold sex from their wives. Heavens, no! The thought never crossed my mind to do it or that other men do. Countless times I have had men voice their angst and frustration to me over the issue of their wives withholding sex from them, never the other way around. Likewise, never has a woman mentioned her husband withholding sex from her. Since we know this is true, it is conceivable that embarrassment or perhaps the conversation being considered inappropriate may have kept the subject at bay. This subject has proven to be humbling, reminding me that my sphere of influence is not as big as I thought.

Focusing back on the husband withholding from his wife, the subject of this section, withholding is very different from being too tired. It is different from feeling under the weather or stressed out after a long day or week. Withholding is different from being preoccupied with trying to do too many other things in a limited period of time. It is far worse than any of that. Why would any man knowingly do this to his wife? I had to find out. From a research standpoint, there are many reasons a husband would do this. According to Psychology Today, "Human beings fear isolation more than any other experience. This behavior threatens abandonment or exile and is severely more wounding to a relationship" (Gunther 2023). Reading between the lines, it is conceivable that some men use withholding to control and punish women. Who wants to feel abandoned and unloved? What wouldn't a person do to avoid this? If a husband is withholding sex from his wife, it only seems reasonable to ask, Where is he being fulfilled?

Gentlemen, to be clear, giving her affection *only* when she asks for it is still withholding. While we may not be guilty of transgressing the letter of the law, we are guilty of transgressing the spirit of the law. If we did not have some issue with her, we most certainly would request or initiate love and affection. Would we treat someone else like this? Would we want to be treated like this? Do we actually think we can fool God? Trying to skirt the command still reeks of sin and no one is being fooled. Have we forgotten that he sees the matter of the heart? We must get this right!

Paul addresses this problem directly in his letter to the church at Corinth. The overarching takeaway is that the husband is always to be considerate of the wife's physical and emotional needs (conjugal responsibility). There are many other supportive verses like Ephesians 5:28–29—we will get into this later—and Matthew 7:12, treating others as we ourselves want to be treated. Paul tells us why, though the thought of it may repulse us, we need to think about it because we are the ones opening the door to sin, and we know sin is waiting to participate.

Paul says the reason to avoid this is "so that Satan will not tempt you because of your lack of self-control" (1 Corinthians 7:5 NASB). In an effort to make this abundantly clear, if we are withholding from our wives, we put her in a position where she can be tempted by Satan to commit sexual immorality against God and us by defiling the marriage. If she commits the sin, our hands are not clean. We are not absolved of our participation in it. Remember the garden? Let us not be deceived—sin comes after as many people as it can take down. Think the scenario through. You are upset with your wife for one reason or another. As payback, you decide you are not going to be affectionate with her for a few days. As with anything, days can easily turn into weeks, and weeks turn into months. See, the thing is, it is not that you didn't want any affection or that you don't miss the affection—you don't want it from her or to give any to her. Where will that attention go (or come from)? There are many women out there just like your wife (make it personal), wanting, needing, and even craving an intimate relationship—in some cases, if unresolved long enough, anyone can find themselves in compromising situations. Rejection and isolation can lead to this even when it isn't premeditated. We should not be quick to think that our homes are somehow exempt or that we have it under control. Take a moment to search the Internet for how many church leaders fall because of immorality. I will make the task a little easier. Limit it to just within the past six years. Usually, these church leaders have considerably more to lose than you and me, yet they succumb to the very same sin, sometimes over and over again.

I really don't like to give the enemy too much credit. When we say, "The devil made me do it," it is probably nothing more than deflection. We are solely responsible for the wrong things we do whether the temptation is from without or within. The other woman "throwing herself" at us does not absolve us from the consequence(s) of our actions. It is us. It is our freewill choice that makes us solely responsible. No one can make us do anything, including the enemy. Please listen: it is not worth it for either party to journey down this road. The implications are far reaching and can be quite devastating, not to mention the potential embarrassment. Moving right along—

Stop depriving one another, except by agreement for a time, so that you may devote yourselves to prayer, and come together again so that Satan will not tempt you because of your lack of self-control. (1 Corinthians 7:5 NASB)

The thing I noticed when I first read this verse is the use of "depriving" (withholding, abstaining) for an agreed-upon amount of time to pray. It's as if God is saying, "Come talk to me for a bit, but don't stay too long because Satan, the great accuser, is waiting around to tempt her. Who has time to think about sex while praying? Well, unless you are praying about sex. It almost seems like an exaggeration — how much time is too long, or are my prayers that short? Am I supposed to be having weeklong prayers? While there is a bit of hyperbole at work, the seriousness of the matter is real and significant.

Here is another jab at self-control. Paul says that if we cannot live as single people with self-control, get married (verse 7)! Why, then, would we get married and force another to exercise self-control by withholding from him or her? I know I said I did not want to deal with the wife's responsibilities but allow me this one because it is important to include it here, though it may be a no-brainer and irrelevant in our situation as married men of God.

Since it is just you and me here, inquiring minds want to know— Have you ever used (or considered using) 1 Corinthians 7:3–4, emphasizing the wife's responsibility, as a way to "encourage" your wife into having more sex? How did that conversation turn out? Probably not so well, I'm thinking. Don't get me wrong—I do understand the intent, and at the outset, reading 1 Corinthians 7:3–4 does seem like a reasonable request for your church-going wife. However, delivery, timing, and how it is received are significant. We should ask ourselves, Is it possible that she might perceive this as a form of coercion? I know, I know. That thought never occurred to you. And how many times have you wound up in the doghouse because you didn't completely think through what you said or did? Maybe you lucked out and she did not think your hurling Bible verses at her was coercive. Instead, she may be considering the hypocritical factor, especially if she knows the Word.

Are you keeping up with all your responsibilities as husband and disciple of Jesus? If not, consider Jesus's own words:

> Why do you look at the speck that is in your brother's eye, but do not notice the log that is in your own eye? Or how can you say to your brother, "Let me take the speck out of your eye," and behold, the log is in your own eye? You hypocrite, first take the log out of your own eye, and then you will see clearly to take the speck out of your brother's eye. (Matthew 7:3–5 NASB)

Before we go hurling Bible verses at our wives (or anyone else), we need to check our own walk with God. When our walk is perfect . . . nah! I still suggest refraining from throwing God's statutes in her face. We must be more understanding and compassionate in our thoughts, conversations, and actions with our wives (and others too. It's biblical. See 1 Peter 3:7; Philippians 4:8; Ephesians 4:29; Matthew 7:12). From just those we should see Bible verse-chucking is not the way to go, and it does not require much discernment on our part to figure that out. Sorry for my digression.

If your wife is withholding from you or has lost interest, you must know adultery is not an option. Under no circumstance is it excusable. This is Christianity 101. Even the unbelieving world tries to live by this standard. But knowing obviously doesn't change the statistics! One more off-topic but very relevant note. Although this applies only to her withholding, that we are not supposed to talk about, I need to talk about this somewhere because it impacts your walk with her and God. What do you do when she is withholding from you and your needs are going unmet? If it is consequential to a short-term issue — she's mad at you, wait it out. You cannot be affectionate with someone that doesn't want your affection. But be ready to resume affection when she comes out of her mood (see 2 Corinthians 5:18; Ephesians 4:32; Hebrews 12:14). If it is long term — Pray. Pray. Pray. Repeat as necessary. You need God's covering. Adultery is not an option. Under no circumstance should this section's opening verses (with the wife's portion in it) be taken to mean that a husband can or should ever force himself on his wife. Forced sex is inexcusable. Yes, contrary to what some might believe, it is rape, and being married is not a permission slip to get whatever you want whenever you want it. "Her body is not her own" is not a pass for you to have your way whenever our heart desires—ever. "Her body is not her own" simply means that she must consider your physical and emotional needs above her own. If forced sex (rape) is taking place or the thought has crept into your mind, you need to confess it before God and repent immediately. Then you should seek the forgiveness from your wife and get help from a qualified individual as soon as possible. Rape is an ungodly act. It is a sin (see 2 Timothy 3:1–7, focusing on verse 3, regarding self-control), and it is very damaging physically, psychologically, and emotionally for her (Pasque 2023).

I like to believe I am a quick learner, so here we go as I do not want to make the same mistake as I made with gender bias and withholding. Men, if your wife is abusing you, see someone. I also learned that this is not make-believe. It does happen.

In closing this section, guys, regardless of how we label it, we need to be sure that our wives get the affection they deserve and need. It is our duty. We are not the master-keepers of our bodies—they are. We must remember affection is not limited to sex but includes many other related needs: emotional support, quality time, care, and concern among others. Because there is no one-size-fits-all definition, we need to take the responsibility and find out how our wives define it. Being a provider for the family is good. However, being just a good provider will get us only so far. Paul reminds us that sin is crouching at the door for its opportunity and that none of us are immune to its effects.

Let's Stay Together

And a husband is not to divorce his wife.
—1 Corinthians 7:11 NKJV

The Bible contains many references to marriage beginning with the relationship between Adam and Eve. While there was no one present to throw rice, or witnesses to sign a marriage license, by the end of Genesis 2 we clearly see the relationship between Adam and Eve is that of marriage, as Eve is referred to as Adam's wife. Later God establishes a relationship with the descendants of Jacob, also known as Israel. The relationship between God and the Israelites is that of a marriage covenant (Isaiah 54). Marriage is used again between Jesus and the church often in what is referred to as the new covenant. This marriage is different in that it is not with a specific people but available to all the world. The price (a type of dowry) was paid not of silver or gold but with the blood of Jesus, the bridegroom (1 Peter 1:18–21). The official wedding celebration is to take place at a future, unspecified date. This is announced in the book of Revelation and in many other places throughout the Old and New Testaments.

The use of this imagery throughout the Bible *and* the fact that the Scriptures teach that God hates divorce should cause us to see the significance in both marriage and divorce alike. Here is what the prophet Malachi is told to speak to the people on behalf of the Lord (note: *garment* is a euphemism for "wife" (Strong, 2001)—

> *"The Lord God of Israel says that He hates divorce,* for it covers one's garment with violence," says the Lord of hosts. "Therefore take heed to your spirit, that you do not deal treacherously." (Malachi 2:16 NKJV, emphasis added)

God has always intended for husband and wife to stay married and committed to one another. We should never lose sight of this, his view of marriage and equally his view of divorce. That is not just initially, as I'm sure not many couples think of the possibility of divorce in the early stages of marriage but rather throughout the later stages of marriage when consideration thereof is more likely. Truth is, we need to make it our view (because it is his) and not settle for simply being aware of his view. This mindset can change how purposed and dedicated we are with getting things right should the marriage ever become less than ideal. It is when things are less than ideal that it is easiest to fix.

Once "less than ideal" progresses to the systemic issue level, it is more difficult to restore.

Divorce is an emotional subject for millions of Christians. It is unfortunate that Christians are not much less prone to divorce than the unbeliever. But that begs the question *Why is that?* I believe it is because marriage is not really discussed, preached, or taught. The same question returns: *Why is that?* Why is it that ministry for couples, if it exists, seems to be an afterthought when compared to other ministries in the church—especially when it is important to God and prominent in the Scriptures. I am not blaming anyone. I am just a curious kind of guy. I knew nothing about marriage as I have come to know it since. At that time I knew even less about divorce. I now know, after the fact, that God *never* intended for a husband and wife to separate.

Consider this for a moment but disregard whether people could/would live as described but whether you agree with the principle of the matter. Imagine a man being a true disciple of Christ and pleasing him is above all else. Imagine a woman being a true disciple of Christ and pleasing him is above all else. Now imagine the two were to get married remaining unchanged in their spiritual walks with God. If they are true to that definition (not their own or others' definition) from a biblical perspective, divorce would never be in their vocabulary. Their marriage and consideration of divorce would be as far apart as the east is from the west. This must be the foundation of every disciple of Christ. I have three questions and answers based on this scenario:

1. Is this possible to achieve?
   Absolutely.

2. Will it be easy?
   No.

3. Will it be worth the effort?
   Absolutely.

Do you agree? I happen to be one of those believers who takes

God at his word. If he says to do it, it can be done. Doing it will be challenging because, as with most of his Word, it is contrary to our natural minds and ways. I also believe that if there is a promised "reward" for obedience, then it is definitely worth our effort. That said, our compliance should never require reward. I make every effort to be obedient because it is the least I can do.

Let's stay with this scenario a little longer. After years of research and my understanding of all that God has for marriage, I am fully committed to the following belief: Arranged marriages "wouldwork" in the Christian faith provided the man and woman are fully committed to walking with God. The two could marry on their own without going on a single date or having met. Their marriage would be successful and the two would have the immeasurable favor of God on their lives. Again, we're stressing the point that both the man and the woman must desire to please God above all else. Did you agree with the first part and not the second? It would be very difficult to imagine myself in that situation but know that I do not intend to apply that to other people and not myself. Removing my imagination of the situation is necessary as I believe this to be an absolute truth.

Instead, many Christians, particularly in the United States, our "what makes Mrs. Right" right has nothing at all to do with God or her commitment to him. Instead, "what makes Mrs. Right" right is driven by our own tastes and preferences, all of which are subject to change over time as our desires and feelings change. *Both* are unreliable yet they are the foundation of many marriages! It is so easy to see why marriages are so vulnerable.

Let me say it this way, as I've mentioned previously, and again it is probably going to upset many of you—but it is nonetheless true. Every divorce is a consequence of selfishness on behalf of *at least* one person, sometimes both. Every divorce happens because one or both do not carry their crosses. At least someone made himself or herself and what he or she wanted (or did not want) more important than the will of God *and* the covenant relationship the couple were in. I have tried, desperately, to think of every possible scenario in which divorce happened purely out of selflessness. Even when we pull back the façade of "It's not you—it's me." we find selfishness. Jesus says that divorce came only as a result of stubbornness (Matthew 19:8). I think selfishness and stubbornness are in many situations synchronistic. Today we do not see divorce as being borne out of stubbornness but a right every married person has. I guess that is true. We do have a freewill choice to do as we desire or to do what we want. Divorce is a freewill choice not to do as he desires.

We live in a do for self, Just Do It, get yours, YOLO ("you only live once"), make yourself happy, get mine, microwave society. Consequently, selflessness is obscure to most. Or at best, selflessness is something we *might* take on seasonally or situationally. It has become a quality relegated to a miniscule portion of society unachievable by most. How wrong are we!

Divorce obviously isn't a new phenomenon. It goes way back well before it is first mentioned in Deuteronomy (also referred to as "put her away"). How can I so boldly make that claim? God created the law to deal with divorce only because people were either already doing it or grumbling about not being able to (and/or perhaps abandonment). This law was not preemptive but was in response to man's stubbornness (Jesus said it – not me).

For New Testament folks, divorce is also addressed here too. Here is the harsh reality of the matter as told by Jesus: "But I say to you that whoever divorces his wife for *any reason except* sexual immorality causes her to commit adultery; and whoever marries a woman who is divorced commits adultery" (Matthew 5:32 NASB, emphasis added). If this is new to you and you're in this position, are you thinking something like "What should I do now?" especially for those who were divorced before *really* committing their lives to walking with God. To you I say this: I believe this is a one-time sin. In other words, sin is committed upon divorce and likewise at marriage to a divorced woman. The divorced couple does not thereafter live in perpetual sin until death. Neither would we live in perpetual sin were we to marry a divorced woman. If we are in this position, we must confess our sin and repent and accept God's forgiveness. Then go about living out the rest of our lives as a grateful disciple—upright and blameless. That said, if we are not divorced, we should not take advantage of his forgiveness by divorcing anyway and then confessing and repenting afterward!

In the new covenant Jesus gives us a single reason for divorce being acceptable in his eyes—sexual immorality. Now for the second and final reason, given to us by way of the apostle Paul. He adds the following: if *because of your faith* your unbelieving wife wants a divorce, it is acceptable to divorce, and we are freed from marriage's commitment (1 Corinthians 7:15). I emphasize "because of your faith" as it is acceptable only when the unbeliever initiates the divorce due to your living for Christ. That said, because I know how folks can be, it would not be acceptable for a believer to overdo church commitments to get the unbeliever to want a divorce. That, my friend, would be ungodly, manipulative, and opportunistic, to say the least.

Recapping, there are only two situations in which divorce is *not* considered a transgression (sin) against our creator:

- sexual immorality and
- because of your faith your unbelieving wife wants out

Did someone ask, What about domestic abuse or neglect? It is sinful for a believer to be abusive to his family. A man taking care of his home is a godly standard for all men of God and not a requirement of only overseers and deacons (1 Timothy 3:4, 12). Notice in those references that managing home and family must be demonstrable *before* fulfilling either of those positions. It is not to be "picked up" when we decide we want the position of overseer or deacon. It is also not something you grow into after taking the role. Let me try it the following way in the event that someone isn't quite sold. When applying for a job, we find a list of requirements for the position. Let's say for argument, one of the requirements for the applicant is that he or she must be able to type 70 words per minute with an accuracy of at least 90 percent. If the applicant types 30–40 words per minute with 60-percent accuracy, he or she need not apply. The speed and accuracy must already be verifiable. It is not something to work up to while on the job. In the same way, managing home and family should not be viewed as mandatory for only becoming an overseer or deacon. All God-fearing men must take care of their homes (their little gardens of Eden).

As for divorcing on the grounds of abuse or neglect, the Bible is not as silent on the subject as many believe. Its position is clear, though we need to read between the lines a smidge. Here is what I mean. We already know what the acceptable reasons are. So by default, we know what is unacceptable—every reason that is not acceptable. When there is an accepted list, there is no need to list what is *not* accepted. If I were to go to a store's checkout and read a sign at the register that says, "Only Mastercard Accepted," is there a reason to list the credit cards that are *not* accepted? No. The person who walks up to the register and asks, "You don't take Discover?" is asking a . . . I won't say it. But I still have a lot more godly principles to talk through that may touch some nerves.

Guys, here is the takeaway. If we are in the place where we are contemplating divorce, we need to reconsider. There is no such thing as too much prayer. We might also try godly counsel. You've already been doing that? Then keep it going while doing everything you can to get right with God and her. Never forget that the favor of God is with us (see Proverb 18:22). If she is contemplating divorce, sometimes all we can do is pray and do the right thing as it pertains to her (and family if applicable). By the way, praying for divorce does not make sense—we already know God hates it. What would be the point in asking for it? We do not want to pray against his will as he is known for giving people over to their sinful desires. That is not where we want to be in our walk with him.

Most of you who are reading this are probably already married and trying to get your lives in order now. You are married to the woman you chose and there is no going back. We understand that "no going back" is paramount. We can see "no going back" as being regretful of our current situation or we can see "no going back" to motivate us to do better than we did. I suggest making the conscious effort to choose the latter.

Paul concludes his unequally yoked position with "But to the rest I say, not the Lord, that if any brother has a wife who is an unbeliever, and she consents to live with him, he must not divorce her" (1 Corinthians 7:12 NKJV), a command for the married man that we will go through next.

*Husband and wife are working together. She is
removing a wall while he assists where he is needed.*

YOU'RE GOOD . . . I'M GOOD

If any brother has a wife who does not believe, and she
is willing to live with him, let him not divorce her.
—1 Corinthians 7:12 NKJV

I considered and reconsidered adding the above verse a time or two. In my
mind I was at war with this being a command, statute, or precept of God
because of Paul's opening words, "But to the rest I, not the Lord, say . . ."
But after a short conversation with my friend Max (thank you, brother), I

am convinced that its inclusion is important to this work. I want all of you to know that I am fully committed to the importance of the entire Bible.

> All Scripture is given by inspiration of God, and is profitable for doctrine, for reproof, for correction, for instruction in righteousness, that the man of God may be complete, thoroughly equipped for every good work. (2 Timothy 3:16–17 NKJV)

My original position was that what Paul says after "not the Lord" is no doubt the right thing to do but may not necessarily be something that God will hold us to. I am convinced that this is a standard God will hold us to if the situation exists, because of our impact on the family. I would like to take this time to substantiate my "flip-flop" for your consideration. I have personally had believers tell me that they should leave their spouses because they (usually the husbands) don't live for God like they do. Their position stands firmly on "because Scripture says we shouldn't be unequally yoked." In other words, the wife feels she is more dedicated to being a Christian than her husband. Well, isn't that interesting? Whenever I hear this statement, and it is quite often, my mind just starts firing off questions in no random order. Who are we to make that call about another believer? Who is to say that if they are weaker that they must live the remainder of their lives that way? Have you always been such a "strong believer"?

One other question I often think is this: *If she is saying that to me, what does she say to her husband? How does she make him feel? Does that motivate him to aspire for greater?* I also feel that the statement seems uncomfortably and potentially close to being hypocritical. Just one more for the road. You do know that Paul was not comparing husband to wife or levels of believers. I could go on, but what I have listed is probably more than enough. If you've used that language, I don't intend any offense. I'm just sharing my inside voice with you and please know that in no way (orally, with facial expression, or with body language) do I communicate those thoughts to the other person. Instead of immediately responding with those and similar thoughts, I listen (see James 1:19).

Let's now go right to verses 14 and 16 of 1 Corinthians 7—the basis for my change of heart. Paul gives us his reasons that as God-fearing husbands we should remain married to unbelieving wives:

- The believing husband sanctifies the unbelieving wife.
- The children are holy and not unclean because of the believing father.
- The unbelieving wife could be saved by the believing husband's presence.

Considering that many are more sympathetic to others only after walking in their shoes for a while, put your wife and children's shoes on right now. Many of us have come to the knowledge of our Lord and Savior because others were praying for us. Think about your life since, or how about your residence in the hereafter had they not prayed? Some of us have come to the faith because others witnessed to us. Where would we be now if they never had? There are some, like me, who hit bottom and that brought us to God. Imagine living the rest of your years freefalling but never bottoming out. What then? You could very well be that positive person for someone in your house! As believing husbands, we have positional power bequeathed by God and the power of influence. What would happen if that were to go away?

In short, yes—this command was of Paul, but it rests firmly in sacrificial living that God calls us to. It is selfish, however we justify it, to walk away from an unbelieving wife. Leaving turns upside down every one of the commands God set in place for his men to do for their wives!

"But if the unbeliever departs, let him depart; a brother or a sister is not under bondage in such cases. But God has called us to peace." (1 Corinthians 7:15 NKJV) According to Paul, only then will we no longer be under bondage and likely free to remarry without causing any new problems. In my opinion, this is an example of Paul loosing on earth what would consequently be loosed in heaven (Matthew 18:18).

Hopefully you will agree that these verses are contextually appropriate with the rest of the book. Because of the power of our presence and the other responsibilities of husbands we should never leave despite thinking that her faith in God, or lack thereof, is reason to leave.

Chances are that if you are a believer and she isn't you will likely (not definitely) experience some travails but remember to stand firm. Keep these things in your mind as they may prove important in your journey—

- In Matthew 10 Jesus says some interesting things. Here is the synopsis: Jesus is working miracles, as usual. He sends out his disciples to preach, heal, raise the dead, and cast out demons. He warns them that persecution will come. Households will be divided but anyone that receives the message, receives God. But he keeps reminding them that despite all of that, not to be afraid. As it relates to this book, I will bring to your attention a few key verses (both from the NKJV).

  Verse 21:

  "Now brother will deliver up brother to death, and a father his child; and children will rise up against parents and cause them to be put to death."

  Verses 34 – 39:

  "Do not think that I came to bring peace on earth. I did not come to bring peace but a sword. For I have come to 'SET A MAN AGAINST HIS FATHER, A DAUGHTER AGAINST HER MOTHER, AND A DAUGHTER-IN-LAW AGAINST HER MOTHER-IN-LAW'; and 'A MAN'S ENEMIES WILL BE THOSE OF HIS OWN HOUSEHOLD.' He who loves father or mother more than Me is not worthy of Me. And he who loves son or daughter more than Me is not worthy of Me. And he who does not take his cross and follow after Me is not worthy of Me. He who finds his life will lose it, and he who loses his life for My sake will find it."

  Now for the takeaway. If there is tension in the home because of your faith, it is not personal. The message of the gospel is an offense to the unrepentant. Your wife is not rejecting you but Jesus. Jesus is warning his disciples that the offense is so strong that it will divide families. What must be understood is that Jesus *is not* teaching hate but the need to be able to separate yourself from even the closest family members should it become necessary.

- Another related message is found in Matthew chapter 12. Here's its synopsis:

Jesus offends the Pharisees by allowing his disciples to pick grain to eat on the Sabbath and healing a man on the Sabbath. He is healing people from the multitudes who followed him. He is casting out demons as well. While he is talking to the people his mother and brothers were outside the gathering but interrupted that they might speak with him.

But He answered and said to the one who told Him, "Who is My mother and who are My brothers?" And He stretched out His hand toward His disciples and said, "Here are My mother and My brothers! For whoever does the will of My Father in heaven is My brother and sister and mother." (Matthew 12:48-50 NKJV)

Here is what we need to glean from that — Jesus redefined "family" as not those of blood relation but those that do the will of the father. That is heavy stuff! If your wife isn't doing the will of God she is not part of your spiritual family. Okay, wait, I am not suggesting that you neglect your responsibilities at home and volunteer for everything you can at the church causing more strife. The point is to persevere in doing the will of God. Your relationship with him cannot be compared to acquiescing to hers.

- Now, for the last one 2 Corinthians 6:14-18.

Do not be unequally yoked together with unbelievers. For what fellowship has righteousness with lawlessness? And what communion has light with darkness? And what accord has Christ with Belial? Or what part has a believer with an unbeliever? And what agreement has the temple of God with idols? For you are the temple of the living God. As God has said: "I WILL DWELL IN THEM AND WALK AMONG THEM. I WILL BE THEIR GOD, AND THEY SHALL BE MY PEOPLE." Therefore "COME OUT FROM AMONG THEM AND BE SEPARATE, SAYS THE LORD. DO NOT TOUCH WHAT IS UNCLEAN, AND I WILL RECEIVE YOU. I WILL BE A FATHER TO YOU, AND YOU SHALL BE MY SONS AND DAUGHTERS, SAYS THE LORD ALMIGHTY." (2 Corinthians 6:14-18 NKJV)

If you are already married this is not your get out of jail free card. We should understand that from the opening verse 1 Corinthians 7:12. These verses address friendships between the saved and unsaved. They are included here because it is important to understand the conflict that can arise between you and your wife because of your faith. If you were single and saved and you wanted to date someone that was not saved, most mature believers would advise against that with these verses as support.

Remember, the ultimate goal is for you to stay together and represent your family to the best of your God-given ability. There could be rough road ahead. If given an ultimatum, my recommendation — choose wisely. On the other hand, and I hope this to be the case, she is fine with your choice though it may not yet be hers. Keep these words from Jesus in mind:

A new commandment I give to you, that you love one another; as I have loved you, that you also love one another. By this all will know that you are My disciples, if you have love for one another (John 13:34–35 NKJV)

There is no need to press her into the faith. Do not separate yourself from her emotionally (marriage covenant violation). There is no need to demonstrate piety or put down her beliefs. All you are asked to do is…just…love…her. Let your love for her be your witness.

BE THE HEAD

The husband is head of the wife, as also Christ is head
of the church; and He is the Savior of the body.
—Ephesians 5:23 NKJV

Another touchy subject! I know—some of these topics are rough but
we want to be on the correct side, right? The husband being the
head or the wife being subject to him can set off very emotional
discussions – okay, arguments. Here is my personal take on it, for what
it is worth. Set this as priority number one—Love your wife as Christ
loves the church. When we do that, it is never about having control
over our wives but being a covering for them. It will never be about
ordering her around just because we think we can, but recommending
a course of action based on prayer, knowledge, and forethought. This
includes taking absolute (full) responsibility for the consequences of
the recommendation, particularly the negative ones as the positive
consequences could come across as prideful, which by the way comes
just before a fall (Proverbs 16:18). We want to practice humility.

How many of us have heard and will rattle off sayings like "Too
many chefs spoil the pot" or "Too many captains, not enough sailors"?
How many realize that too many heads of the house cause division in
the home? God designed it so that there is one head of the house, and
that person has a greater burden than the other members of the house.
The head does not do everything but is responsible for it all. It is a fact
that men are indeed the head and will always be, and it is not limited to
the culture of a bygone era. Again, it is not about flexing authority or
might, but it is about there being a point person on whom God places
responsibility.

Here I go again with my examples! For those who were raised
with siblings in the house, can you recall an older sibling always being
left in charge? Or in the case in which you were the oldest, I am sure
you can remember being asked why a younger sibling did something
he or she should or should not have done on your watch. Who took
one for the team? I bet you did. Being in charge has its benefits and
liabilities. Unlike our parents taking away responsibility and giving

it to another younger, more responsible sibling, God is not going to do that! He is leaving them with us and will hold us accountable for them.

After God created Eden, he left certain responsibilities with Adam, one of which was taking care not to eat from the tree of the knowledge of good and evil. Notice in the garden, whom did God first confront after eating of the fruit? Let's have a look.

> Then the eyes of both of them were opened, and they knew that they were naked; and they sewed fig leaves together and made themselves loin coverings. They heard the sound of the Lord God walking in the garden in the cool of the day, and the man and his wife hid themselves from the presence of the Lord God among the trees of the garden. *Then the Lord God called to the man,* and said to him, "Where are you?" He said, "I heard the sound of You in the garden, and I was afraid because I was naked; so I hid myself." And He said, "Who told you that you were naked? Have you eaten from the tree of which I commanded you not to eat?" (Genesis 3:7–11 NASB, emphasis added)

When God showed up on the scene, it seems clear that Adam and Eve were present. Yet God confronted Adam first even though Eve had started their descent into sin. Adam had disobeyed a direct command. When God questioned both of them, he already knew the answer. He wanted them to stand front and center to give an account for their disobedience. But both had only worthless responses to give.

In like fashion, we marry, we carry full responsibility for the home (our garden of Eden). In the end, we are going to give an account for the things that did not comply with his directives. In your house your wife may be better with fixing things. You might be better with the cooking or cleaning. We were provided with help because God knew we would need it. He knew that we would be at our best with our wives by our side. As I previously stated, your wife *is* your equal! Working together demonstrates wisdom and oneness. But we must never forget that we are still responsible for making sure that the operation gets done and done correctly. If one of us isn't responsible for paying the bills, that does not mean we don't have conversations about the budget and know what it is (and stick to it!). If no matter how hard we try we cannot wrap our heads around financial planning but she can, that does not excuse us from the retirement planning process—no Pontius Pilates here (see Matthew 27:24). We do not get to stick our heads in the sand. Should something go wrong in our little garden, it was on *our* watch!

My wife is far more organized than me. I am not disorganized— she's just significantly more organized and in more ways with many more things. If either person has this tendency, it should be great for the marriage. If we were both like me, some things might not necessarily get done in a timely way because it has something sitting on top of it. It only makes sense to us for her to do what she loves to do and do so well. On the other hand, it would not be ideal if we were both like her. Between the two of us, someone would probably label the dogs and file them away. Balance is a great thing. I believe we keep each other from going too far to the "dark side," either side.

Listen—we *need* to get this. As husbands it may not cut it that we are not good at or have no interest in certain things. What happens if our wives also couldn't care less about the same things? They need to get done and it is our burden to carry. Additionally, we cannot and should not try to do it all. Marriage was not designed with that purpose. It means we must learn to work with our wives, and that includes communication.

How we treat our wives falls under a few other sections in this book and is very important here. For some of us communication will be quite challenging. For others, not so much. Some of the challenges we face can come from our personality. Others may come from hers. Nevertheless, we still need to work together to accomplish things. Tone and body language are all part of communication. On the job it may be possible to make demands. At home, that may not be the case. But even if it were possible, should we? I believe it is best practice to speak with our wives as we would want to be spoken to. Yes, that's pretty much what Jesus said. While we are responsible, she is not our underling or personal assistant. If we don't like orders barked at us from anyone, do not bark orders at her. I'll do you one better. If you don't care about how people talk to you, care about how you talk to her! Do not delegate because you think you have a right to. Ask for help because you need to. That is who we are designed to be for each other.

That was not a mistake. Eve was created to help Adam. We all know that. But few realize Adam was also helping Eve. He was doing the things he was created to do that she was not. The God-ordained way for husband and wife to get everything done is by assisting each other. Here is a suggestion: Every time you ask something of her, do not ask because you feel the work is beneath you. The perspective we need to have is asking because God said we need help. But that works in the inverse. She needs our help. Make yourself available to help regardless of what the situation requires. That means learning to do the things she usually does. Yes, especially those things you think are woman's work! There is no woman's work—there is only work in and around the house. We know that we will ultimately be held accountable for it. There are a few things only a woman can do, and those were God-given assignments, *not* husband-given!

The way we communicate with or treat our wives will come back to us, either in the form of something good or the form of something bad. It is God's law of sowing and reaping. This is referred to throughout the Bible, but I really like the way the prophet Hosea uses it: "Sow righteousness for yourselves and reap faithful love" (Hosea 10:12 HCSB). Paul is less colorful with it and goes right for the gut: "Don't be deceived: God is not mocked. For whatever a man sows he will also reap" (Galatians 6:7 HCSB). If we sow barking orders, condescension, and superiority, we will reap discord, resentment, and hostility. We can best believe God's Word; we will answer to him for it. If we push—in some way, her own way, she will push back. You may not intend any ill will but let me tell you—perception is real. Always consider how you speak with her. The Bible warns us to avoid even the appearance of evil (1 Thessalonians 5:22). I am continuing to learn from experience that I need to stay on top of this in my own life. Sometimes my delivery is too dry or direct and can be understood in ways that I never intended. The consequence of that misunderstanding comes back to me in ways that leave me confused. I have learned that if she takes something I said the wrong way, the problem was in the delivery, *not* with the reading. Stay vigilant—it makes a huge difference!

Here is one of marriage's paradoxes that many of us must learn to masterfully navigate. Women will say that they do not want to be told what to do. Yet the very same women will say they want a man who can stand firm and not be easily walked on or rolled over. In the past I have often asked myself, *How does that work exactly?* Experience has taught me that it just takes *patience* and *understanding*—two familiar words found sprinkled throughout this text. The key is to learn that "you have to ask me nicely." I am confident that Jack Nicholson and the writers of the movie *A Few Good Men* had no idea how powerful and useful those words would be. When you get good at it, you can ask without the accompanying question mark—a request. Here is an example of a request (an ask-without-the-question-mark but short of a demand) that if delivered the wrong way can cause problems. The missus is on her way somewhere and we say, "Text me or call me when you get there." A reasonable request, right? For many of us the purpose behind that request is to fulfill the need for knowing she got to her destination safely. I don't make that request every time she walks out the door. First, because I don't need to know every time. Second and more important is that it could easily come across as being controlling. We need to use good judgment and discretion before we speak. Think about it—she drives to work every day. She visits her mom. She goes to the market. In those situations, a request like that may not be necessary. However, when she is going to a WNBA game with her friends and has to drive through a sketchy part of town (where they always seem to stick these venues), "Text me when you get there" would be an acceptable and reasonable request. This shows concern and not that we have a need to be in control. That is how you set a request with courtesy and respect, something she will be honored to uphold. That same request formulated as a question is weak and sounds optional when we don't want it to be. If she doesn't do it, it's not her fault but her taking the option not to. That is walked on, perhaps rolled over when that happens too often. *That* is the type of man most women do not want.

It is interesting to listen to men talk about this subject. Most gloat over this verse as if it has anything to do with superiority and entitlement. It does not. This is a prophetic consequence for Eve's disobedience. God frequently uses, "Because you have done this . . ."

To the woman He said: "I will greatly multiply your sorrow and your conception; In pain you shall bring forth children; Your desire shall be for your husband, *and he shall rule over you.*" (Genesis 3:16 NKJV, emphasis added)

As men we should understand that God gave dominion to both man *and* woman to have over all else (Genesis 1:27–28). When he says to Eve "And he shall rule over you," men, please understand that this was not a blessing but a prophetic consequence. As time progressed, men did just as God foretold over many millennia ago—they ruled over women. What history reports and what we see today is not what God designed for man and woman at the end of creation on the sixth day! *This* new thing, his ruling over her, was not "very good." God spoke this as he was doling out his divine, righteous judgement and prophetic insight consequential to their disobedience. God knew before time that the male ego and chauvinism would rear their ugly heads. This curse would be a problem not only for her but also for him. Again, history shows the resulting indifference, fighting, and injustice between men and women. The more recent fight for women's equality isn't new and it will continue. Jesus said, and some of us know by experience, that a house divided against itself cannot stand (Mark 3:25). Discord and resentment have brought about an outright pushing-away of men, and the evidence thereof is all around us, getting stronger as time passes. Do you see the parallels between men and women in these words from Jesus?

> Jesus called them to Himself and said to them, "You know that those who are considered rulers over the Gentiles lord it over them, and their great ones exercise authority over them." (Mark 10:42 NKJV)

What is interesting, as Jesus continues, is that we are probably seeing a picture of the relationship between man and woman before the fall, something you and I can try to live out now in this fallen world as husbands.

> Yet it shall not be so among you; but whoever desires to become great among you shall be your servant. And

whoever of you desires to be first shall be slave of all. For even the Son of Man did not come to be served, but to serve, and to give His life a ransom for many. (Mark 10:43–45 NKJV)

Adam would have served Eve, and with Eve being equal, she would have served Adam. This is where we need to get to in our walk with our wives. As with many other topics in the Bible, the worldview is in complete opposition. To the world, serving represents weakness or is an indicator of positional authority in which those in the lowest tiers serve the higher. As believers, we should understand that this too is a lie of the enemy. Serving demonstrates humility and self-sacrifice. This is the love of God! There is honor in serving others. There are internal feelings of reward. Imagine if today, instead of looking in the most bizarre places for a new way to feel good, people would instead serve one another. What a wonderful world this would be! What actually takes place instead is the desire to be served on every level down to some children serving the whims of professionally, socially, or economically frustrated parents. It does not end there. I have witnessed older siblings forcing younger siblings to serve their needs, mimicking what their parents do to them. It is all so twisted. But we can do better. Dare I say, we *will* do better. Guys, it starts with us.

As we all know, because of man's choices, beginning with Adam and Eve through today, we are all living in a state of disrepair. It will remain this way until Jesus returns and rights everything. Until then, we need to understand what we must do. As Christian husbands, it begins with being in right standing with God. We need to know what his precepts are, and we need to be in a place where we can communicate those commands to our wives where applicable. In other words, we must be prayerful, studied, and have both wisdom *and* understanding (there's that word again). When God directs husbands to do something, we have to be sure to communicate that to our wives and be sure she is in a place to get there. The purpose for this is that we need to be able to present our wives to ourselves as faultless, just as Christ is preparing the church for himself at his coming (Ephesians 5:23–28).

Do not be prideful in this position. As Stan Lee said through his comic book character Spiderman, "With great power comes great responsibility." Here is the way King Solomon said it: "A man's pride will bring him low, but a humble spirit will obtain honor" (Proverbs 29:23 NASB). As husbands, our position is a badge of honor we wear with respect. Humility is not a sign of weakness but one of strength. Pride is its antithesis.

In too many Christian households this is a problem. As husbands we can do only what we can do. Hurling scriptures at her will not resolve this matter. This is another one of those examples of the importance of staying prayerful, walking in his statutes, and remembering that her compliance has no bearing on our being godly representatives of our homes.

THE BLUEPRINT

Husbands, love your wives, just as Christ also
loved the church and gave Himself for her.
—Ephesians 5:25 NKJV

This verse speaks of a love that is not fleeting. It is not conditional. It is not based on feelings. It is not the love that gives us butterflies in the stomach. It is not the love that makes us want to stay on the phone all night because we don't want the conversation to end. Please don't misunderstand me. That type of love is erotic love, and it certainly has an important place in marriage. But what God calls us to here is very different — so much more. The love commanded here is an enduring love. It has nothing to do with feelings but is more like a state of existence. It does not change or diminish. This love requires vulnerability yet is incredibly strong. This love takes work to accomplish and does not come into existence "at first sight" — it is built over time. Too many of us want the butterflies–in–the–stomach love. It is easy. It is fun. It is a feel–good love. Buying chocolates, flowers, cards is erotic love. We feel good. She feels good.

As we've all probably discovered, erotic love is not sustaining. I don't believe it was ever meant to be, by design. It has purpose but cannot carry the full weight of life's issues when they start to fall like heavy, wet snow does in Tug Hill, NY. The love that God calls us to is like an underground bunker — where both husband and wife find refuge. In it are the things needed to sustain marriage over time. While I have heard and read erotic love described as a lower type of love with enduring love being a higher form, I won't jump on that bandwagon because I believe both are equally important. We need to use both types of love in intervals — like wind sprints. After a period of erotic love switch back to focusing on building the enduring love for a longer period of time. Don't forget to focus back on erotic love! When we do these at varying intervals we are "strength training" both – 1 Corinthians 7:3 love with the type of love found in most other places in the Bible.

I am of the opinion that this single command of Ephesians 5:25 given to husbands is probably the most challenging of them all. By that, I do not mean the act of loving but more so getting a clear understanding of what the duties entail. In other words, how does one love as Christ loves the church? Looking back at what we've covered so far—having only one wife, being sure to address her physical and emotional needs, not divorcing, and taking on all the responsibilities of headship—aren't as broad and comprehensive as this. Neither are the responsibilities following. Think about all of the things Jesus does for the church! How do we love anyone else like that? Others may be asking, "Can we?" Of course we can! If it were not possible, it wouldn't be a command but an example of manipulation and cruelty. We know that *is not* our God! Think about the guy being coerced to work above capacity with the planted idea that he would get a management position. In reality either he is not the candidate, or the position does not (and will not) exist. This command is not that. It is not a carrot on a stick, and neither are the others.

Jesus's love for the church (us) is multifaceted and complex. We must *really* dive into the Word of God for direction, that we might be compliant. In light of that, I believe what we do find would be a fraction of how much Jesus actually does for his bride. For one, there are things that should, could, or would happen to us if it were not for his intervention. How do you list what you cannot see? Perhaps we can chalk that up to intercession. Obviously we are held accountable for those things. I am just making the point that what he does is without bounds. I do believe that when we are walking in obedience and doing all we can do, he will do the things we cannot on our behalf.

When we study the letters to the seven churches (Revelation 2–3) we see just how multifaceted his love is. But before we take a look at the letters, we need to look at and understand something *very* important:

> The Revelation of Jesus Christ, which God gave Him to show to His bond-servants, the things which must soon take place; and He sent and communicated it by His angel to His bond-servant John, who testified to the word of God and to the testimony of Jesus Christ, even to all that he saw. Blessed is he who reads and those who hear the words of the prophecy, and heed the things which are written in it; for the time is near. (Revelation 1:1–3 NASB)

The father gave it to our Savior, who gave it to an angel to give to John, for all of his servants. And for what reason? So that *every* subsequent generation would be prepared. Prepared for what? His return. It is clear that the reader and hearer who take heed to all that is written therein will be blessed.

We are able to glean some very important messages from the first three chapters of Revelation. In them we find a "report card" for seven churches. From a very high level, anything deeper would be beyond the scope of this book, let's together see what we find that points us to methods Jesus demonstrates his love for the church. While some may say they disagree with how I have categorized the verses, that is not the point of this exercise. What *is* the point is that we are clearly shown the love of Christ for those that believe on Him. His first demonstration of his love for the church is the fact that he provides us with a warning. We cannot overlook that fact. He loves us so much that he tells us what we need to do using other churches as examples. Here are some others…

- Watching over us (2:2, 9, 13, 19; 3:1, 8, 15)
- Praise (2:2, 3, 6, 13, 19; 3:4, 10)
- Advice/direction (2:5, 16; 3:3, 4–5, 11, 18, 19, 20)

- Warning (2:4–5, 10,14–15, 20, 22–23, 25; 3:1–2, 3, 11, 19, 16–17)
- Reward (2:7, 10, 17, 24, 26–28; 3:5, 8–10, 12, 20–21)

How does all of this serve as an example as to how we are to love our wives? When we know the Word of God and see anything in what she says or does that does not line up correctly, where applicable we are to mimic Christ. I am not making this up. Look back at the verse. It says, "Love your wives, just as Christ also loved the church."

I hope it is just as obvious that every step in this self-sacrificial work needs to be done in a loving manner (1 Corinthians 13:4–8). Will she like the steps you take? Probably not immediately, and even if realized later that this was a loving gesture, we may never get a thank you. But regardless of her response, our objective is not receiving accolades or expressions of appreciation but to be obedient! We cannot worry/obsess over perceptions but be sure to be compliant with God's love definition. If we are confident that we were patient, kind, and so on in dealing with our wives, her response, if not in God's love, is entirely between her and God. We can only do *our* part!

It is also worth mentioning in Jesus's example he never comes across in a condescending manner. Our wives are not children, underlings, or incapable thinkers. Even when giving "praise" we need to be careful how that is delivered. Everything matters.

Here is another example of Christ's love for the church—Ephesians 5:25–27). We see that our relationship with him serves as an example in that he sacrificed himself, he sanctifies and cleanses, that he might present us without having spot or wrinkle or any other blemish. I would like to draw your attention to the end of Ephesians 5:25 – *and gave Himself for her.* I'll break that down succinctly using language most of us will recognize. Ask not what marriage can do for you but what you can do for your marriage! Guys, being a husband is self-sacrificial. It is not work best achieved while beating one's chest and grunting.

I do want to begin our dive into 1 Corinthians 13:4–8. While this is applicable to all of our God-given precepts, this one in particular makes use of the word *love.* What is love? Did the song by Haddaway and/or the SNL skit with Chris Kattan, Jim Carrey, and Will Ferrell pop into your mind? Every time I proofread this section, the skit and the song play in my head. I digress.

As we get into this, I have a few questions. Is love measurable? In other words, is it possible to love someone a lot or just a little bit? Can I love a person more today than I did yesterday? Is it possible for love to change over time? Can a marriage be full of love at the outset but over time become loveless? I will oftentimes say that I "love" butter pecan ice cream. Some people love the smell of mothballs or the smell of gasoline (petrol). Some will say that the moment they saw their significant other, it was love at first sight. How about that new car? How often have you heard or said, "Oh, I just love my new car"? The list of questions can grow days long.

When we use or hear the word *love* in our everyday lives, its context often makes it subjective. I can love someone or not love them. Some women can feel loved when they receive flowers or cards. Some feel love when they get gifts. Some men feel loved when they are respected.

The word *love* is definitely overused and consequently many times undervalued or unappreciated. I don't believe the problem is inherent to the word itself but that the same word is used across varying degrees of intensity and meaning. Sometimes *love* is a more convenient word indicating how much you really, really, *really* like something. It's quicker! In other words, in some cases it is also quite possible that *love* and *like* are used synonymously.

Here's one use of love that happens more than I believe we would admit—feigning love in order to get something we might not otherwise get. That is completely disingenuous, manipulative, and is contrary to God's definition of love. Does Jesus love his church in the same manner as we love wearing jeans? I certainly hope not. With all these questions, how is it that we are to take Jesus's commandment in the Bible that we are to love one another?

An unscientific poll of church-going Christians would have you believe that what differentiates God's love and the love we say to one another is that his love is unconditional. While that is true, it's woefully incomplete. Paul describes love to the church at Corinth also for our benefit.

> Love is patient, love is kind, it is not jealous; love does not brag, it is not arrogant. It does not act disgracefully, it does not seek its own benefit; it is not provoked, does not keep an account of a wrong suffered, it does not rejoice in unrighteousness, but rejoices with the truth; it keeps every confidence, it believes all things, hopes all things, endures all things. Love never fails. (1 Corinthians 13:5–8 NASB)

Having that description, we are now able to safely conclude at least three things. This kind of love is the kind of love Jesus has for his bride, the church. This is the love we as men are expected to live out through our wives. Last, this is not at all the same love that we have for our favorite movie (or anything mentioned earlier for that matter). Unfortunately for us, the same word is used.

The kind of love Paul speaks of is powerful and it does not quit. The God kind of love does not vary. It is not situational and neither does it waver or fade over any length of time. It is not subjective. Understand this: the God kind of love is definitely achievable. This is the type of love you and I need to be aiming for and keeping in our marriages. This is the type of love God will use to measure our love for our wives.

All that I have written thus far, I believe, barely scratches the surface of the love Jesus has for the church, which we are to have for our wives as well. Some may question how we can use an unknown to measure a known. It's easy. If our love for our wives is given when she does this or does not do that, that would be measurable love. That is not the love we are striving for. Why do we tend to overcomplicate things? Perhaps it's just me. Men, we do not need an itemized list of examples of Jesus's love for us. If only we would remember to do two things: (1) love God with all our hearts, minds, souls, and strength, and (2) love our neighbors as we love ourselves. I've mentioned a few times in this book that loving God above all else is essential to our success in loving our wives as he mandates. The moment that the focus of our attention is no longer God, that is the moment we begin to run aground. I believe that by our reading of this book for its intended purpose means we are on our way. As we die to self and its desires, we are then in the best place to love

God and our wives as he desires. The second is not a new requirement for us as it overlaps our next command—Ephesians 5:28–29.

Here is one more example of loving like Christ — he didn't come to be served but to serve. Gentlemen, this is a huge step in our call to be loving husbands. Jesus is our example. We are not in the position we are in to be served but to serve. I am sure some of you are in really tough marriages as such this command will be challenging to live out. In the last section we talked about this being contrary to society. But I will bring it closer to home. It will prove difficult to serve when it is not appreciated or reciprocated. Who wants to feel undervalued or be taken advantage of? I get it. But the truth lies here: our negative experiences with others cannot keep us from our walk in obedience to God. What matters is that we are doing and will keep doing what we are to do—because we love God. What anyone else does in return is between them and God. They *will* have to answer for it. As I have said before and will say many times again, just do your part. That is all we are responsible for and that alone is more than enough.

In the closing of this section there is one more very important thing I want to mention, and as I have often done earlier, I am going to use an example. Have you ever played the game "Spot the Difference"? If not, I will explain it briefly here. Two images are placed side by side. Usually the image on the left is the untouched original while the image on the right has been modified in different places. The object of the game is to find all the differences in the image on the right usually within a specified amount of time.

Imagine this: at the day of reckoning standing before the great throne of our God, our Savior and Advocate seated to his immediate right. All the heavenly hosts are in their designated positions. Our almighty Father is sitting majestically on his throne. He bellows, "Lower the screens!" Out of nowhere, to his left, two massive screens lower, quietly and effortlessly. After being fully extended, the left screen displays all that Christ is doing and has done for his bride. The Father continues, "Show my son's (that's you and me) relationship to my daughter (our wife), his bride." The right screen awakens to life at his command. Here is a question we must always think about: Will there be any differences between his image and mine? (See 2 Corinthians 13:5.)

99

MIRRORED LOVE

> Husbands ought to love their own wives as their own
> bodies; he who loves his wife loves himself. For no one
> ever hated his own flesh, but nourishes and cherishes it,
> just as the Lord does the church.
> —Ephesians 5:28–29 NKJV

Reverting to the end of the last section, "Love like Christ," this section's verses give us two more examples of Christ's love for the church: he nourishes and cherishes her. Because we are to love our wives as Christ loves the church, we should get those two added to our responsibilities as husbands. But what does it mean to nourish? How does it work when you are talking about nourishing someone else?

Perhaps like me, when you think of *nourish,* you think of eating high-quality foods that provide for the health requirements of your physical body. Is Paul suggesting that we need to make sure our wives are eating properly? While I would say that is a good thing to do, I believe Paul's admonishing is more substantive. Again, I'm not saying that eating food having good nutritional value isn't important—it is. Let's flesh out Paul's greater intent, however. To do that, we will look at another verse that uses the Greek word for *nourishes* from the verse above - *ektrephō* (pronounced ek-tref'-o).

"And you, fathers, do not provoke your children to wrath, but *bring them up* in the training and admonition of the Lord" (Ephesians 6:4 NKJV, emphasis added). Both the words *bring* and *up* are *ektrephō* in the original Greek. Clearly this has nothing to do with healthy eating habits. The words *nourish, bring,* and *up* all refer to the effort exerted to raise to maturity in terms of growing—not physically but mentally, emotionally, and spiritually. The intent of these two verses amounts to doing what we must to bring our wives and children to maturity as it relates to their relationship with God. That would involve teaching, training, modeling, and so on. This cannot be done if we do not know the Word and live by it ourselves. Suppose you began your walk with Christ as a family and all of you are new to the faith. Are you necessarily in a position to help someone else mature? The best thing to do in this case is to seek a

Bible–believing and Bible—teaching church. The problem with that is that it presupposes that you know what that looks like. Relieve yourself of the pressure. Prayerfully bring your concerns to God. While doing so, you need to make sure that you are diligently seeking him through his Word. I believe it means spending more time in the Word than anyone else. Commit to reading, studying, and praying. Where you are deficient, grace abounds! Before you realize it, you will be able to answer questions, intercede for your wife and children, and sift what comes into the home with your newly formed biblical worldview. As you nourish yourself in the Word, nourish your wife likewise. This aligns us perfectly with God's command to us through the apostle Paul. *Cherish,* on the other hand, deals more with physical and emotional care. *Warm, tender,* and *affection* are all colorful synonyms.

Originally the heading for this section was "Love for Self = Love for Wife." I had no idea that heading would be understood by others in ways other than what was intended. I would later battle with the question "Should the title of this section be flipped to 'Love for Wife = Love for Self'" instead?" Is there a difference? Depending on who you ask, the answer might be an emphatic yes! The exchange I had with others only underscores the simplistic brilliance in these verses. If I read this as being "The level of love needs to be either raised or lowered to match the other," then I've missed the message. This is not about "how much" love I give. Neither is it about similarity, but sameness. Quoting the late Lane Smith from the movie *My Cousin Vinny,* "Identical!" There are no ebbs and flows—it is always on and exactly the same. As Jesus said, when anyone has seen him, he or she has seen the father. Similarly, when others see the love I have for myself, they are looking at the love I have for my wife. So as with a mirror that reflects an identical image back to the viewer, that self-love is mirrored in her.

Whenever I read the opening verse, I am reminded of Adam's statement "This is now bone of my bones, and flesh of my flesh." Though not physically taken from us, woman is part of man. The two together are a whole. Separately they are incomplete subsets. I believe that if it were possible to poll every married man anonymously with the question "Do you love your wife," the overwhelming response would be yes. If I ask him if he loves himself, I believe the overwhelming response would still be yes.

How many would say that they love themselves more than they love their wives? Or looking at the inverse, how many love their wives more than they love themselves? While that sounds great, it is unbiblical and raises the question in my mind, "Is that even possible?" God's desire is that the love be the same, not imbalanced, as honorable as the latter may initially sound. If it is possible to love our wives more than we love ourselves, we need to start loving ourselves more so that the love is the same—not love her less to match our lower level of self-love.

I believe that "God created us to love ourselves" can be used as a template for how to love our wives. As a Christian, with a biblical worldview, I believe self-love to be one of the "self" prefixes that is actually good. Again, it is not really about self for the self, but a measure for how we are to deal with others. Self-love should never be confused with narcissism. Narcissism takes self-love to the extreme, and by its very definition a narcissist cannot love another equally. Narcissism is an ungodly character trait. Generally speaking, it seems to be the case that society has an over-inflated view of self. Without any exaggeration, people will walk across the street without regard for oncoming traffic, the traffic light, or the pedestrian crosswalk. The pervasive mentality seems to be *I dare you to hit me.* People will cut in front of others instead of waiting in queue. People blare their music without regard to anyone else. I have no idea why I am surprised to witness these things, as I am an avid student of eschatology. Paul warned us that in the last days perilous times would be evident:

> For men *will be lovers of themselves,* lovers of money, boasters, proud, blasphemers, disobedient to parents, unthankful, unholy, unloving, unforgiving, slanderers, without self-control, brutal, despisers of good, traitors, headstrong, haughty, lovers of pleasure rather than lovers of God. (2 Timothy 3:2–4 NKJV, emphasis added)

There is a sense of entitlement that I have never seen before that places the self above everyone else. Taking this further, this entire section inspired other sincere thoughts. I felt conflict with the entire reading and those who self-harm or attempt/commit suicide. If you have not noticed yet, because of my apologetic background, I tend to look for questions that others may throw at me in an effort to trip me up. It is my way of preparing a defense for what I believe to be true (see 1 Peter 3:15). With my being entirely convinced that God's expectation of us transcends time and all cultural influence, how am I to understand and explain this? So I did a little digging and found some information to share with you in case other inquiring minds want to know. As it relates to self-harm, not a single credible source (that I could find) ever makes mention of self-harm being related to self-hate. Self-harm seems always to be a consequence or manifestation of other mental and emotional issues.

Another person might ask, "What about those who have contemplated or attempted suicide? Are you saying the Bible says they should love others when they don't even love themselves? Again, in order to get a better understanding of the subject, I did some digging. It doesn't seem to be the case that suicide is like self-harm. Most research suggests that suicide is an act of selfishness, a consequence of other mental disorders, or even side effects of some legal drugs. According to Merriam-Webster, by definition *selfish* is—

• concerned excessively or exclusively with oneself: seeking or concentrating on one's own advantage, pleasure, or well-being without regard for others
• arising from concern with one's own welfare or advantage in disregard of others (selfish n.d.)

Listing the following synonyms (from Merriam-Webster also): *egocentric, egotistic, narcissistic, self-absorbed, self-centered, self-concerned, self-infatuated, self-interested, self-involved, self-loving, self-obsessed, self-oriented, self-preoccupied, self-regarding, self-seeking, self-serving.* Yes—not a single descriptor that confuses the issue; *selfish* is in direct opposition to this verse and too many other commands to list here. To no surprise, God's omniscience and his track record remain undefeated!

I do feel compelled to address those who have been directly impacted by suicide (or feel/felt suicidal). Please know that the information above was not with the intention to offend. I cannot imagine the depth of loss, though I can relate to having those feelings, as many do, at one time or another.

Hopefully you were able to understand the purpose behind my research and why I included the results—never being that I might cast the first stone.

Continuing . . . guys, think about this for a moment. You know we love ourselves a lot. We are always looking for ways to please ourselves. We buy new stuff for who? Us! Some of us take care of our bodies (even to the extreme) as well as our minds through diet, vitamins, and games. We eat. We clothe ourselves. Most of what we do we do because we love ourselves (not in a bad way but as God expects us to).

Maybe you are going through a tough time, and consequently not in a good place to think about self-love. Try thinking about how much *you think* your wife loves herself. Imagine her giving you as much love as you think she loves herself. How would that make you feel? Take the time now to imagine that kind of love being expressed toward you—daily, without end or strings. Can you see it? Okay, good. Now flip it. That is the kind of love God wants us to give to our wives! Remember: these directives are *for* you and not *about* you. Therein lies the paradox. While this sounds as though everything is all about her and you feel confident, none of this will be reciprocated. It is not *really* about her. This is about God and being obedient and our love for him. When we chisel that truth into the brain, it makes living the life of a husband easier and even rewarding.

Personalize it. Because of my obedience, God will love on me in ways I could never imagine, a love without bounds. His love continues in the afterlife — because he is love. God's love has to be our incentive. While God cannot love us any more or any less, the demonstration of that love most certainly can be more or less evident. Again, I stress—be obedient out of love for him, not for its return. That is not to say we will never get the love we might want from our wives! Usually we receive what we give. It is a law of God—sowing and reaping. When loved upon, most women will drop their walls and love back in ways we can never imagine. God said her desire will be for you (Genesis 3:16). Here's a suggestion: *live a life deserving of her love.*

Below is a short list of questions I have had other people speak with me about or I have asked myself at one time or another. Mind you, some responses are coarse and very direct. I will not make an excuse for them; neither will I apologize for my directness. When I look out the window and see all that is going on in the world, I am reminded that I need to be sure I am rooted and anchored. Whether it is the coming of our Savior or my appointment with the end of this life, I do not know which is coming first or when. I need always to stay ready. I do not want a preacher, teacher, or author to sugarcoat anything. I get more than enough sugar elsewhere—with dental fillings to prove it. Give it to me straight and that is what I feel compelled to do with this book and especially here.

Be careful with Ephesians 5:28–29 and always remember that this command is not at all the same as reciprocity. This is giving and doing regardless of any return.

Q. What should I do when my wife does not want to be near me because of something I said or did?

A. The love that God wants us to give our wives is not exclusively based on physical love (sex, hugging, kissing, and so on). Therefore, her disposition is irrelevant. There are many more ways to demonstrate love. Continue those. Do not let anything keep you from loving her as you are told. Obviously, one of our assignments may not be possible for some time and that is 1 Corinthians 7:3–4. As it relates to this question, remember this: we must always be ready for reconciliation (Matthew 5:23–24; 6:14–15: Ephesians 4:32; 6:15; Colossians 3:13; Hebrews 12:14). Spend some quiet time in prayer and self-reflection. As we learned earlier—not too much time! In the meantime, keep yourself in the right mental, emotional, and spiritual space. Think on those things that keep you from getting pulled in. Whenever she is ready, resume the physical loving and conversation. Hold no grudges. Do not seek vengeance.

Q. What do I do if she loves with differing levels of physicality than I do?

A. How does Christ demonstrate his love for the church? Not physically! There are other ways of communicating love that do not require touch. But in an effort to answer the question directly, revert to the "golden rule," as it was called in early elementary school. Do unto others as you would have them do unto you (Matthew 7:12). If you want your preferences to be honored, then honor hers. It might turn out that she finds that attractive, increasing her desire for you and physical love with you. But do not do it hoping for something in return. Do it out of obedience to God's mandate.

Q. What if I am not feeling particularly loving today?

A. Does the command qualify itself with "based on how we feel"? Doing the right thing when we would rather do something else is what makes parts of this walk challenging. It is largely about doing the things we may not necessarily want to do and doing the things we may not want to for the people we feel are least deserving of it. This is the epitome of carrying one's cross (the sacrificial life). We need to do it when we least feel like it. That will make it even easier to do it when we want to. Before we realize it, the right thing is always being done.

When we correctly understand that our wives are part of us a shift will take place. Read this out loud to yourself. No really, I am serious. Go to a private place and read this next section out loud so that you can hear it.

- When someone speaks ill of my wife and hurts her, it hurts me too.
- When my wife is frustrated because of people on the job, it frustrates me too.
- When my wife is stressed out because she has too many things on her plate, I feel stressed too.

You can stop reading out loud now. Have you ever noticed when someone speaks ill of their wife you start feeling dismissive toward him – even when it's your friend. I don't mean talking through a frustration but "dogging them out." I believe this happens because the two are to become one is written on our heart. That internal "code" causes us to react emotionally when it is violated. That code gives us the understanding that not only is he talking bad about her, but he is also talking bad about himself. Let's make it personal. Have you ever vented to someone about your wife in frustration and walked away feeling worse. You mentally and emotionally squirm draped in this feeling you cannot shake. It is because venting all that stuff was antithetical to your God–ordained walk with her. Talking about her is hurtful to her and by default – you. Stop talking about yourself like that! Love her like you love yourself. If you feel like you don't love yourself then you need to love her like you need to be loved because you are both in drought. But where do you get that love if you think you don't have it? Truth is, you do have it. You have either forgotten about it or don't realize it contextually because we all have it. You get it from reading your Bible. You get it from thinking about your story. Where you came from. All of the things you did in the past. For some, even the things you are doing now. Don't stop there because that can make you feel worse, justifying your downheartedness. Continue with thinking about a God... No, *the* one and only true and living God that loves you despite all of those things. The God that left an infinitely beautiful heaven with all power and walked this miserable planet. The God that was verbally and physically abused *before* the cross. Then was lifted up and died for you because he loves you!

For a lot of us, when our wives are feeling hurt, frustrated and stressed – being task–oriented – we want to jump to problem–solving mode. That is a blessing in some situations and a curse in others. Many of us are wired to think, here is a problem that needs fixing. Then we start mentally building a list of the five, seven, or ten things we need to do to fix it. Find your private space again and read the following out loud.

- Not every problem can be solved by a checklist.
- Not every problem is for me to solve.
- Every problem deserves my attention.

When she is going through things be there for her emotionally, mentally, and physically. Pause the game. Put the paper down. Turn off the buffing machine (be sure to put the lid on the carnauba wax though). Listen. Empathize. Love. Then pray with her and for her. God most definitely can address your woes. I mean her woes. Oh yes, that's right they are exactly the same!

Before I close this out, I do want to say one more important thing. Some things our wives go through are God–ordained. In this walk – as God develops us – he will break us, reshape us, and then use us (repeating cycle). We do not want to pray against that but that his will be done with her as it is done in heaven. Sometimes we have to go through the fire for the dross to rise and be skimmed off the top and discarded. This is good – painful – but good. If you don't have a solid biblical foundation, prayer life, and know your wife well, you will not be able to discern between stuff to deal with and God at work. I am convinced that without those three things, a Christlike marriage shifts from merely having its challenges to being outright difficult.

This kind of love is the kind of love that breaks down barriers/walls that exist between husband and wife. Walls we are responsible for from past wrongs and walls others have built that she now carries. For the most part, every section in part four can break down walls.

Couple is in his house. He is stripping wallpaper. She is helping with cleanup.

BE SWEETER

Husbands, love your wives and do
not be bitter toward them.
—Colossians 3:19 NKJV

"Do not be *bitter* toward them"? What does *that* mean? To answer that, let's take a little bit of a dive. Sure, we could go straight to a dictionary to figure that out, but we want to know what the author, Paul, intended first, then go from there as necessary. This method of study is paramount to gaining an understanding of the Scriptures. The dictionary does not always convey the message the author intended for the reader. Therefore, to rely on today's dictionary definition could prove erroneous.

In Greek the word for *embittered* is *pikrainō*. It is from the word *pikros,* which literally means "sharp," or figuratively "acrid." It is used in two other places in the Bible: James 3:11 and James 3:14. In verse 11 bitter water is contrasted with sweet water, and that is the basis for the title of this section. However, in verse 14 James gives us a little more (verse 13 is added for contextual clarity):

> Let him show by good conduct that his works are done
> in the meekness of wisdom. But if you have bitter envy
> and self-seeking in your hearts, do not boast and lie
> against the truth. (James 3:13–14 NKJV)

The word *but* in verse 14 is a contrasting coordinating conjunction. If you remember from your English classes back in your middle school days, a conjunction joins two or more phrases together that are both of equal importance. In this verse it is quite clear that James is saying that meekness of wisdom is not possible if there is bitter envy and self-seeking in the heart. Now watch this: *both* of these characteristics are in direct opposition to the love we are to have for our wives (1 Corinthians 13:4–5). So far we know from his own words that bitter is the opposite of sweet. We also know that it is in opposition to love.

In the original Greek, *pikrainō* is defined as "bitter." Yes. this was the roundabout way of finding out its meaning using the same English word. It doesn't always work out that way. Nevertheless, according to Merriam-Webster, using only the relevant meanings, *bitter* is—

- distasteful or distressing to the mind
- vehement
- exhibiting intense animosity
- harshly reproachful
- intensely unpleasant especially in coldness or rawness (bitter n.d.)

While we are at it, for the sake of clarity (making sure you and I are reading from the same sheet of music) before we further develop this section, let's see how Merriam-Webster defines *vehement* and *reproachful*. Vehement: marked by forceful energy, intensely emotional (vehement n.d.). Looking at the root word of *reproachful*, which is *reproach*, we get an expression of rebuke or disapproval and a cause or occasion of blame, discredit, or disgrace (reproach n.d.). Ouch!

Here's the truth. *Anyone* can find himself or herself feeling embittered at any given time. When we are overly focused on something that someone does or says to us, we can unwittingly respond with embitterment. We can feel embittered towards others because of preceding stressful events. Yes, sir! When we are having a bad day, we can treat others in an embittered way. Hopefully those are "one-offs" and not the norm. When that behavior is uncharacteristic, we should be able to quickly apologize and clear the air. You know, sometimes things happen. While embittered responses may come out in the heat of the moment, Paul is likely not talking about the one-offs, though we need to fix those. I think he is talking about something more—ongoing attitudes and responses. This is far more detrimental to her, to each of us, and our marriage (and family where applicable). It is that ongoing embittered attitude that is sinful. We should understand that one-off embittered responses in their infancy often gestate to become ongoing attitudes/dispositions, a reason we are not to let the sun go down while we are still angry (Ephesians 4:26). Have you ever had "the pleasure" of running into an embittered person at work or at the register? Or how about at church? If you don't know what I mean, I am talking about the person causing everyone's body language to shout, "Oh, no!" when he or she comes around. Imagine the wife, kids, or the dog seeing you in that manner! Mate, we do not want to be that person. God forbids it and makes it clear with this command.

Here is another related verse to meditate on: "Let no corrupt word proceed out of your mouth, but what is good for necessary edification, that it may impart grace to the hearers" (Ephesians 4:29 NKJV). We can add to that, among so many others, "A gentle answer turns away wrath, but a harsh word stirs up anger" (Proverbs 15:1 NIV). There are embittered dispositions and embittered words, and both take their toll on the recipient and with us. Neither of these are how we are to conduct ourselves, in or outside the home. While it may be true that we may not use embittered or corrupt words, an embittered disposition usually comes first. When we find ourselves stressed out over bills, our job, feeding our families, or where we are going to live, they can quickly become heavyweight burdens affecting our countenance—yes, most times without our notice. But I assure you: others notice it. We must take these concerns of ours to God in prayer (1 Peter 5:6–7).

When we live according to his precepts, we must have confidence that he will take care of whatever our concerns are. He created and sustains all that exists from those things within reach and beyond the deepest areas of space that we can barely fathom. Surely he can handle whatever comes our way (regardless of how great it seems in our minds). We must understand that giving it to him does not mean that we are to ignore situations we find ourselves in. Bring them to him, and as we will discuss later in part five, test him in all that he promised. If we are lined up properly in our walk to receive his promises, he will come through.

To our own detriment, we men do not usually seek out and rely on others who we can share our burdens with. This means we are more likely to carry the stresses of life unnecessarily on our shoulders. I have a micro-network of godly men around me whom I can bounce things off of. However, my go-to is my wife. I have no problem showing vulnerability because there is no one better designed to help me with my concerns. I will admit, it has not always been that way. This came as a result of putting greater attention on becoming one flesh. Come to find out, I don't have to pretend to be Superman. She demonstrates compassion and understanding in every case by either doing something to help or saying the right words. Imagine that—another win for God. He knows what he is doing! I find that she is better equipped to help me given that she knows me and my/our situation better than anyone else.

I have come to realize that rarely do my concerns amount to anything, and in those situations I give thanks to God. I may never know what he orchestrated behind the scenes to resolve my problem, but I am confident he did something. It may have just come from my being obedient in walking with my wife. While I cannot answer that definitively, I can say this with surety—I actively pursue being sweeter in both speech and action toward my wife. Doing so has turned so many things around. Being kind and thinking kindly changes the way the words come out of my mouth. In turn, she doesn't need to guess what my tone means. The more I practice this, the more I realize how it changes our interaction with each other. Looking back, I see that the overwhelming majority of my communication problems came from something outside of us that happened to me, affecting my tone that in turn impacted her perception of the whole situation. I should have practiced this years ago!

Up to this point it should be clear that husbands must be aware of how we treat our wives, what we think of our wives, and even how we speak about our wives. We need to talk about something that isn't quite as clear but if left unrealized does extensive damage to our relationships with our wives and no doubt with God. I believe this thing is the carbon monoxide of marriage. It creeps in, fills everything, the body loves it, but silently kills everything around it.

I would guess that everyone has at least something they prefer done a certain way. That "certain way" we consider the right way and every other way, wrong. I'll throw myself under the bus here with a preference of mine. On some walls in some rooms there are a bank of light switches (two, sometimes more). I have this "thing" about having all the switches flipped in the same direction. If you have some working knowledge of switched outlets and two-way switches you can probably anticipate my self-imposed conundrum. If you do not understand, I must explain so that it makes sense otherwise it will be difficult to understand the point we'll get to shortly.

I have two walls in my kitchen one with two switches together – controlling ceiling and undercabinet lights (2-gang). The other has three switches (3-gang) – controlling ceiling lights, undercabinet lights, and the hanging light in the kitchenette. Sometimes I need to walk a couple of times between the two walls flipping them to get the "right" combination so each bank of switches is in the same direction. Not too awful, right? Now for the third switch on the one wall. Not only does it control lights in the kitchen, but it also controls the hanging light in the kitchenette. When the kitchenette's light is off and it is different from the others, I need to fix it. I have to go to a third wall and flip the two-way switch that is also connected to the overhead light in the kitchenette. Now six light switches are all in their "acceptable" position. Wait, it doesn't end there. On the third wall there are switches to the outdoor motion sensing light that must stay in the on position. There is a switch that controls a light on the wall outside the patio door. There is yet another switch controlling an outlet. Keep in mind the single switches must be in the up position in order to use the light or outlet. Argh! I feel compelled to make them right. Unfortunately for me I cannot make them all right. Which means when I look at one wall (intentionally furthest away) I have to accept that they are mixed. My wife couldn't care less about any of that as I presume most of you don't either, but I ask you this question — *is it right for me to impose my preference on my wife?* Sure, I could talk to her about "my issue". Pay careful attention to the difference between "my issue" and "my issue with her." There is a huge difference! I should never force compliance with my will on her. If she does not comply I should never hold that against her. This could present itself as me not talking to her because I am angry or frustrated because she doesn't comply. It could manifest as vindication — not complying with some preference of hers out of spite. Now watch how these things can fester and grow to become a silent killer. Every time she uses a switch it affects the way I deal with her. Continued anger and frustration can lead to distance which can lead to direct violation of God's laws (Genesis 2:24, 1 Corinthians 7:2–4, Ephesians 5:25, Colossians 3:19, 1 Peter 3:7 — just from this book).

On the flip side, if my wife has an "issue" with my socks turned inside out when tossed in the hamper, I should not frustrate her. I should try to make sure my socks are in the hamper with the right-side out. If you are thinking to yourself *this is not fair* — you're right, it isn't. This is part of what living with our wife in an understanding way entails. This is also how to treat others as we want to be treated (see Luke 6:31). News bulletin: a self-sacrificial life isn't fair nevertheless we are called to live it. Your reward, at the very least, awaits you in heaven.

Here is something else to consider and it is just as serious—

> People were also bringing babies to Jesus for him to place his hands on them. When the disciples saw this, they rebuked them. But Jesus called the children to him and said, "Let the little children come to me, and do not hinder them, for the kingdom of God belongs to such as these. Truly I tell you, anyone who will not receive the kingdom of God like a little child will never enter it." (Luke 18:15–17 NIV)

What does that mean? Have you ever noticed that children accept almost anything without much pushback? Think about the nonsensical stories of Santa, the Easter Bunny, the Tooth Fairy — and the one that lasted longer than all of those for me — Groundhog Day. It took many more years before I realized we will always have six more weeks of winter and the groundhog's shadow has nothing to do with winter or any early spring. Kids accept many things out of this thing we devalue as we age called trust. They don't accept things because they are not smart or gullible. This is why even the brightest kids fall victim to human trafficking — someone violated their trust.

In the noted verses above, Jesus is saying that unless we are able to come to him with trust we will never enter into the kingdom of God. Let's talk about the adult mindset briefly. Adults do not usually think innocence until proven guilty and that is why we need to be reminded of that in court. We challenge many things because we think we know what's best. With God, we need to accept the message of the gospel of Christ without hindrance or needing it to meet the scrutiny of some natural standard. The gospel is supernatural — working outside natural law — therefore it cannot be explained in the natural.

Connecting some spiritual dots, I hope at least most Christians are familiar with Jesus's statement that if your hand, foot, or eye causes you to sin cut them off or gouge it out (Matthew 18:8–9). From it we should understand that if certain relationships result in our sinning, end them. If we get angry after consuming alcohol, stop consuming it. It is better to lose those relationships and alcohol and go to heaven than continue with either and go to hell. But in Jesus's context, he is talking about anyone causing other believers to stumble.

> If anyone causes one of these little ones—those who believe in me—to stumble, it would be better for them to have a large millstone hung around their neck and to be drowned in the depths of the sea. Woe to the world because of the things that cause people to stumble! Such things must come, but woe to the person through whom they come! (Matthew 18:6–7 NIV)

Woe, in the Greek is an exclamation of grief. Jesus uses this often in the gospels and what followed was never good news. Meditate on Jesus's words above for a moment before continuing. When we impose our own will on our wives (and other believers), it puts a stumbling block in their path. How's that you ask? Let's connect another dot. I think doing so will show a dangerous correlation.

In Jesus's day, he had a particular issue with the Pharisees that relates to this discussion. They imposed their own commands — in opposition to God's — upon the people. This was a huge problem that could be seen throughout the gospels. We cannot go into all of this too deeply here, but I encourage you to read those grasping not only what they were doing to the people but what Jesus's response to them was for doing what they did — not good. When we force our wives to abide by our will, we are burdening them with our regulations. When they do not live up to them — like the Pharisees — we punish them in our own way. Our reaction to her then forcibly puts her in a place where she must be careful not to respond in a way that will cause her to violate God's commands. It is a potential stumbling block for her. If she does not stumble good for her, but we are still on the hook. If she does stumble, woe to us!

Okay, I thought I was finished but there is more. Jesus also speaks against those that wrongfully judge others. People tend to leave out the word "wrongfully". When we project our regulations on our wives and they fail to live by them, our reaction to them — putting it bluntly — is condemnation. Yes, we judge wrongfully because it has nothing to do with a spiritual matter, then we condemn them with our words, by not speaking to them, by withholding — all those things we talked about earlier.

Going back to my light switch preference — do you see how easy it is to fall out of the will of God, over something as infinitesimal as the position of a light switch? I purposefully used a ridiculous and extreme example but prayerfully consider your own preferences in its place. Maybe you have an issue with your wife because her meatloaf doesn't taste like Mom's. Maybe your wife doesn't treat you like your friend's wife treats him. The issue you have with her could be her driving. You think she needs to drive like you do and you let her know it. We need to look at ourselves and we should go to God in prayer to be sure there is nothing we're missing.

DRINK FROM YOUR OWN CISTERN

Marriage should be honored by all, and the marriage bed kept pure, for God will judge the adulterer and all the sexually immoral.
—Hebrews 13:4 NIV

In our effort to live by this "code" of Hebrews 13:4, we should take care not to split hairs. While the verse seems to draw a line around "the marriage bed," in no way should we take it to mean that every place *but* the bed is fair game (the back of a minivan, the restroom on the interstate, or any other available place or space of convenience). Believe it or not, some men feel they can sleep with other women as long as they don't violate the home. It is a real thought, as if it is more honorable. While the letter of the law is met, the spirit of the law is well off course. Regardless of the setting, it is adultery—and God will judge it accordingly.

Again, I will confess ignorance here and share information with you that I never knew. You do not have to go through any embarrassment by asking about it or admitting to it—I'll take one for the team. If you did not already know, the sin of adultery is not limited to the married person. Regardless of the willing participant's marital status, *both* parties are guilty of adultery. Guys, that means not only would we be adulterers were we to have a sexual relationship outside of our marriage, but whoever indulges with us also commits adultery, regardless of her marital status. Taking it one step further, if we withhold our marital status from the other woman, she is nevertheless guilty in the eyes of God. We see this in action when Abraham crossed paths with King Abimelech in Genesis 20.

According to the Bible, Abraham's wife, Sarah, was a desirable and beautiful woman (Genesis 12:11, 14). The Bible recalls for us two incidents when she was taken from Abraham for the purposes of having sexual relationships with other men. The first recorded offense was made by an Egyptian pharaoh (Genesis 12). Pharaoh's officials took Sarah in order that she would become one of Pharaoh's concubines. Because of this, God struck Pharoah and his home with plagues. Get this: Pharoah had no idea the two were married because they pretended to be siblings. To God ignorance was not a valid excuse. Sarah and Abraham did not learn from their deceit and in a later event pretended once again to be siblings. The second time involved King Abimelech, and this is where we find an even harsher execution of justice by God.

> God came to Abimelech in a dream of the night, and said to him, "Behold, you are a dead man because of the woman whom you have taken, for she is married." Now Abimelech had not come near her; and he said, "Lord, will You slay a nation, even though blameless? Did he not himself say to me, "She is my sister"? And she herself said, "He is my brother. In the integrity of

117

my heart and the innocence of my hands I have done this." Then God said to him in the dream, "Yes, I know that in the integrity of your heart you have done this, and I also kept you from sinning against Me; therefore I did not let you touch her. "Now therefore, restore the man's wife, for he is a prophet, and he will pray for you and you will live. But if you do not restore her, know that you shall surely die, you and all who are yours." (Genesis 20:3–7 NASB)

After King Abimelech returned Sarah to Abraham, undefiled, God lifted his judgment on the king, his wife, and his entire household and permitted all of them to live. God's judgment came in the form of no one being able to conceive. That is, the king's household, including his servants, were not able to have children. How long did God's judgment sit on the king and his people in order to realize there was a problem? Take a second to mull over both situations. Neither Abimelech nor Pharoah served God, yet God's judgment fell on those whom we might consider innocent. While I have not heard of such events happening today, we should not believe this was serious only in that day or only because Abraham and Sarah were involved. God is unchanging and he is impartial. While it may seem as if we are getting away with sin today, the staying of his judgment is only a testament of his love, mercy, and longsuffering. At some point, that will end as he must deal with sin because he is just, holy, and righteous. Regardless of the sin, now is the time to stop, confess, and repent while the ability to do so is available to us.

Guys, adultery is a very serious violation with God. We see from both situations that every participant is subject to God's judgement. Scriptures teach that God will no longer put to death the children for the sins of their fathers and vice versa (Deuteronomy 24:16). But that does not say that our decisions cannot cause hardship for our children or others. When the sin of adultery is uncovered, its effect is felt well beyond the two who are engaged in it. If the sin is not exposed, while it might seem that no one is aware, God is very aware. Aside from that, there may be no way of knowing what damage an affair will have on anyone and everyone within our sphere of influence (on both sides!).

This is regardless of what another woman says she loves to do that is not done at home. Regardless of what another woman says that is not said at home. We need to get to the place where we know *no one* is worth putting ourselves and our loved ones in such a precarious position. If you find yourself in this situation now (and/or in the future), take "the way out" God provides. If you have passed all the way outs and have been in it so long that he has given you over to your desires, I plead with you—get it right. Do it now. If not for yourself, do it for everyone else around you. Despite any condition we may find ourselves in, adultery is not justifiable. A wife who withholds, has a long-term illness or disability, or an "open marriage" are not exemptions.

Here is another point I wish to make: "But whoremongers and adulterers God will judge" (Hebrews 13:4 KJV). In the NASB it reads, "For fornicators and adulterers God will judge." God groups these "infractions" that he might address them together. Now is the time to talk about fornication since it butted itself into our conversation. Fornication is the act of having sex with another woman while not being married to her. A "quick fix" or a "one-night stand" are fornication—sins in the eyes of the Lord. Contrary to societal norms, having sex even if there is an informal commitment between the two is fornication. An unmarried couple living together and having sex is sin and it is the sin that keeps on giving. Every day or every year that the two have sex, it is a commission of sin. For those who are unaware, in the Bible fornication is grouped together with sexual immorality (or immorality).

Admittedly, there is something in all of this I am not entirely clear on, and regardless of where the answer lies, we must avoid them both. We know that adultery is a sin. We know that fornication is a sin. We know that God will adversely deal with both. We know that if a married man has a sexual encounter with a single woman the two commit adultery. Here is the question. Does adultery also include the sin of fornication? It would be true that the two are having sex while not being married to one another. That's like getting a flat tire on the highway and while changing the tire being struck by another car. Or falling off a ladder while cleaning the gutters then having the ladder fall on top of you as you lie on the ground writhing in pain from the fall. But that's not all! You will be out of work with no pay. Insurance and unemployment won't kick in until later. Now the family will be feeling the consequences!

According to 1 Corinthians 6:9–10 and Galatians 5:16–21, we know that fornicators and adulterers will not inherit the kingdom. Guys, in these letters *to the churches* Paul is not pointing his finger comparing the lives of those outside the faith to those within it. How can I be so sure? Please allow me to answer a question with a question. Would someone of the world inherit the kingdom if living his or her entire life chaste? Absolutely not. While there are many more verses we could refer to as proof, I'll go with just two that come from our God and Savior directly from a conversation he had with Nicodemus:

> Jesus answered and said to him, "Truly, truly, I say to you, *unless one is* born again he cannot see the kingdom of God.... Truly, truly, I say to you, *unless one is* born of water and the Spirit he cannot enter into the kingdom of God. (John 3:3, 5 NASB, emphasis added)

Full stop. There is no need to look for any other supporting verses as they would be nothing more than overkill. Being that only the born-again has access to the kingdom, Paul cannot be talking about the world but rather those in the faith committing the sin.

As believers we should be impartial when it comes to sin. We need to see them all as transgressions against God. Today Christendom is quick to attack everything else going on in the world but seem to be inoculated against adultery and fornication. I am not being pious. I am writing with a pointed finger but making sure I am included! I am guilty of having favorite shows that promote these sins. Do I turn the channel or get up in disgust? No. Is that right? Probably not, because I believe consistent exposure, especially through a form of entertainment, slowly dulls the senses. There is danger in dulled senses when it comes to the commands of God. Dulled senses are the pathway to acceptance.

All too often I hear the expressions "God knows my heart," "God accepts me as I am," and "God made me this way." Those are not wild cards to be played that will excuse/permit our living outside of his will. Furthermore, each of these and others like it are not fully thought out before saying them with such pride and confidence.

What do the Scriptures say about the heart?

- "*The heart is* deceitful above all things, and desperately wicked; who can know it?" (Jermiah 17:9 NKJV, emphasis added)
- "He said, 'What comes out of a man, that defiles a man. For from within, *out of the heart* of men, proceed evil thoughts, adulteries, fornications, murders, thefts, covetousness, wickedness, deceit, lewdness, an evil eye, blasphemy, pride, foolishness. All these evil things come from within and defile a man.'" (Mark 7:20–23 NKJV, emphasis added)

In our Savior's words, "Every good tree bears good fruit, but a bad tree bears bad fruit. A good tree cannot bear bad fruit, nor can a bad tree bear good fruit" (Matthew 7:17–18 NKJV). How can someone claim to be a good tree while bearing bad fruit? According to Jesus, it is not possible. And what will God do with a tree bearing bad fruit? Again, in Jesus's words, "Every tree that does not bear good fruit is cut down and thrown into the fire" (verse 19). Okay, so let's pretend together verse 18 is not there. By their speech it seems they are saying they are a good tree bearing bad fruit. Let's say hypothetically that it is possible for a tree to bear fruit that is different from itself. According to verse 19, if the fruit is bad, it does not matter what the tree is—it is going into the fire.

Only God knows what is truly in the heart and it is possible for us to deceive ourselves. Hopefully it is apparent that the statement *God knows my heart* is not a solid argument for that use case although it is a true statement. What I think the person who says this is trying to communicate is that God knows the person's best intentions even though he or she might do something else. Although this may be more accurate, it nevertheless results in fire. We are to be doers of the Word, not hearers only.

Next excuse: *God accepts me as I am*. Again, true. However, an important and expected outcome of salvation is that we *grow* in him. The number of verses that support this statement could write its own book. For brevity I included only a few for you to get you started.

- Although too long to type here, it is a heavy weight that I must reference here: 2 Peter 1:3–11
- "Grow in the grace and knowledge of our Lord and Savior Jesus Christ. To Him be the glory both now and forever. Amen." (2 Peter 3:18 NKJV)
- "My brethren, count it all joy when you fall into various trials, knowing that the testing of your faith produces patience. But let patience have its perfect work, that you may be perfect and complete, lacking nothing." (James 1:2–4 NKJV)
- My beloved, as you have always obeyed, not as in my presence only, but now much more in my absence, work out your own salvation with fear and trembling; (Philippians 2:12 NKJV)

Hopefully it is apparent that God's expectation is for believers to grow, to put away those things they were saved from and live a renewed life in him. The Bible teaches that "the wages of sin is death" (Romans 6:23). We cannot save ourselves from death by our works or any other way (James 2:24). Only God can save us—we just need to accept his salvation in all of its fullness.

Last but certainly not least, *God made me this way*. This is not an accurate statement, much less is it a good position to take. In no way did a perfect, loving God create man to sin. Our sin nature is of our own doing, and it started in the garden. Sin continues to this day and into the future until God comes and makes all things right. God has demonstrated that he has given some of mankind over to their own desires, meaning that he has allowed them to practice ungodliness (Romans 1). God did the same many times with Israel (Psalm 81:12). If I were a betting man, though I'm not, I would bet that today the very same thing is taking place. The unrighteousness we see so prevalently may be a result of God allowing people (Christians, that is—I am not talking about the world) to do the unrighteous things of their own heart's desires.

I want to take a look at something together. Matthew 5:27–28: "You have heard that it was said, 'YOU SHALL NOT COMMIT ADULTERY'; but I say to you that everyone who looks at a woman with lust for her has already committed adultery with her in his heart" (NASB). Many verses allude to the harsh reality that our actions follow our thoughts (for example, Proverbs 23:7). Even the secular world is in full agreement with this. How many times have you heard your favorite artists, musicians, or athletes say that at one point they just made up their minds that they would be the best and most successful in their fields, and then it happened? Essentially their achievements are a consequence of thinking about being the best or being successful. Almost all of them make similar statements. Along the same vein, when we lust after a particular woman in our mind, adultery can often follow. We pursue that which we desire and it seems to start in our heart/mind. Am I saying that even if physical sex never takes place, it is still adultery? Yes, because Jesus said it. He said adultery was already committed in the heart. To this day there are certain television channels I cannot watch, places I cannot visit, and people I cannot associate with. I know where my heart can take me if left unchecked. Why waste my time and energy putting myself in the situation where I am forced to check it? Or to always be on guard? No! I have more important things to do with my time. If there is something that causes me to sin, I do all that I can to avoid it altogether (Matthew 5:29).

Another elephant in the room. What about pornography? This is a problem many men face at one time or another. Although sex is rarely ever had between the viewer and the "model," it should still be considered sin based on Jesus's words. Pornography can definitely lead to sin, and it is also consequential to other sins (lack of self-control). This is a hard one in that many of us look at images and videos because we are trying to resolve urges without actually physically being with someone. While it might seem that looking at someone you will likely never have access to cannot be sinful, this view contradicts Jesus's words. It is just a dangerous slope as it can create lust, and viewing it can be in response to lust already in the mind. Pornography usually falls under the umbrella of sexual addiction, and overcoming it varies from person to person. If you no longer want to be a slave to it, do whatever you have to do to get in and remain in God's favor (Matthew 5:27–30).

Now we are triangled in. Wall number one: our demand surpasses her supply. Wall number two: no other women. Wall number three: no pornography. But wait—there's more. What about self-stimulation (masturbation)? Let me say this: there are some in the faith who believe masturbation is a sin because of the following report in Genesis. It is a little long, but when clipped for brevity, the context is lost. Here is the account:

> At that time, Judah left his brothers and went down to stay with a man of Adullam named Hirah. There Judah met the daughter of a Canaanite man named Shua. He married her and made love to her; she became pregnant and gave birth to a son, who was named Er. She conceived again and gave birth to a son and named him Onan. She gave birth to still another son and named him Shelah. It was at Kezib that she gave birth to him. Judah got a wife for Er, his firstborn, and her name was Tamar. But Er, Judah's firstborn, was wicked in the Lord's sight; so the Lord put him to death. Then Judah said to Onan, "Sleep with your brother's wife and fulfill your duty to her as a brother-in-law to raise up offspring for your brother." But Onan knew that the child would not be his; so whenever he slept with his brother's wife, he spilled his semen on the ground to keep from providing offspring for his brother. What he did was wicked in the Lord's sight; so the Lord put him to death also. (Genesis 38:1–10 NIV)

Here are some important points: (1) Judah commanded his son Onan to have a child with his now deceased brother's wife, Tamar, so that the family line would continue. (2) This was a customary responsibility in that day. (3) Onan slept with Tamar but *on every occasion*, before orgasm, he would pull out so that she would not get pregnant.

Folks, this has *nothing* at all to do with masturbation. To tell men not to do this because of this situation is twisting the entire story. And to what end? It is as scripturally sound as saying people should not play board games because we are to avoid factious people. Neither makes any sense at all! Unfortunately, this correction doesn't quite take us off the hook. What most definitely is a problem is that masturbation is at odds with God's command that we practice self-control. "For God hath not given us the spirit of fear; but of power, and of love, and of a sound mind" (2 Timothy 1:2).

While we might think *sound mind* means "sensible" or "sane," the Greek word *sōphronismo* is a bit more complex. "Literally, this word means saving the mind through admonishing and calling to soundness of mind and to self-control" (Strong 2001). It comes from the word *sōphronizō*. Strong's says the following: "This word denotes to be of sound mind, to recall to one's sense, restore one to his senses, to moderate, control, curb, discipline, to hold one to his duty, to admonish, to exhort earnestly" (Strong, 246). Does it sound like a person lacking in self-control is the same thing as saying that person is not acting sensibly? Here is what the same verse in the NIV looks like: "For the Spirit God gave us does not make us timid, but gives us power, love and self-discipline."

Although this is not an actual command, this is what the Bible says about us if we lack self-control: "Like a city whose walls are broken through is a person who lacks self-control" (Proverbs 25:28 NIV). As Thelma from Scooby-Doo would say, "Jinkies!"

October 7, 2023, will go down in history. It is the day that Hamas penetrated Israeli defenses through makeshift tunnels. The Joe Biden administration in the United States will also go down in history as droves of people from various places around the globe were allowed into the United States without recourse. When any territory loses its protections, anything can happen. Both of these situations are examples of what the Bible tells us is similar to the one who lacks self-control.

> I Paul say, walk by the Spirit, and you will not gratify the desires of the flesh. For the flesh desires what is contrary to the Spirit, and the Spirit what is contrary to the flesh. They are in conflict with each other, so that you are not to do whatever you want. But the fruit of the Spirit is love, joy, peace, forbearance, kindness,

goodness, faithfulness, gentleness and self–control. Against such things there is no law. Those who belong to Christ Jesus have crucified the flesh with its passions and desires. Since we live by the Spirit, let us keep in step with the Spirit (Galatians 5:22–25 NIV).

In short, we are not to gratify the desires of the flesh—we are to live with self-control. Masturbation is of the flesh and practicing it seems to fall under a lack of self-control. And while there are still other verses that mention self-control, sober-mindedness, and restraint, I don't feel the need to add more injury. So let's continue. I would feel comfortable with making this categorical statement: more people have sex for pleasure than those who do so only to procreate. Does that mean that most of us operate almost exclusively in the flesh? I don't believe so. When Paul says that we are to render to our wives the affection she needs, we can confidently say that this has nothing to do with a need to have children but a need for intimacy apart from that. So then, when does sex move from a natural desire to something consequential – a lack of self-control? I truly believe it is when it crosses from the natural source, wife, to anything that replaces her for whatever reason. It does not matter what, where, when, or how the urge is satisfied. If it is not from our wives, it is something that is not meant to do what she can. It comes as a consequence of a lack of self-control. Now, the whole "sane" thing tripped me up for a bit, and then I started to think about it more. While that urge is at the bottom of the stockpot boiling up to the surface, think about where that urge takes your mind. What are you thinking about? What are you willing to do? This is where I think the idea of the sane mind comes into play.

This subject brings to my mind the prefix *anti-,* as in *antichrist,* "in Christ's stead." It is not the same as the preposition *against.* When I was writing this, it kept coming to my mind, that everything used in place of our wives is "antiwife." Well, that shines a spotlight on the whole matter! The use of any antiwife is a result of a lack of self-control and consequently sin. Using an antiwife is akin to dropping all your defenses so that anything and everything can get through. In this light, this is why we need to do everything reasonable to abstain from using an antiwife, whatever it may be. This would be wall number four, gentlemen—self-control. We are no longer in a triangle but a cube. Ugh! But it's for our own good.

Did someone ask, "Is there a point in time when we lose self-control? What if we can hold off for a month, six months, a year?" Whoever asked that question, you are probably not going to like my answer. Self-control is self-control only when you are in control. When you give in to whatever that thing is, you no longer have self-control. I have not knowingly eaten beef of pork since 1992. I loved beef so much that I had triple cheeseburgers long before they were ever a thought in fast food. I ate beef at every opportunity given. Loved it! I would later find out that my cholesterol was at a deathly number. With that news, shortly thereafter I never ate it again. I knew moderation was not an option for me. I use that situation as my go-to when I need to stop doing something. I feel that if I can stop eating meat, I can do anything. Pretend the flame-broiled-burger restaurant was actually still flame-broiling their burgers. If I were to walk by and decide to buy one, I would have lost control. I cannot say that I have control—I gave into that thing I was trying to control. Self-control does not work like that. In the same way, I fight against all antiwife urges. If I give in, I have lost control. When I lose control, it is sin and displeasing to God.

I am sure some are thinking this is easier said than it is to put into practice. That is true. If it were not so, statistics would certainly show us differently. Unfortunately, they do not. There are many cases of infidelity and pornography use and abuse that we have all heard about through the news or tabloids. Prominent people in the faith continue to fall as newsfeeds report of their indiscretions. I believe that this is the reason the Lord's Prayer includes "lead us not into temptation"—because temptation is a rough one.

While we diverged a bit from keeping the marriage bed pure, the subject raised other related concerns. Had I left it at just addressing not sleeping with other women, that would leave the possibility that I believe other "antiwives" are fair game. That was something I could not afford to let pass by. I appreciate your patience. And speaking of patience—

PATIENCE AND HONOR

Husbands, likewise, dwell with them with understanding, giving honor to the wife, as to the weaker vessel, and as being heirs together of the grace of life, that your prayers may not be hindered.

—1 Peter 3:7 NKJV

First Peter 3:7 is another one of those verses in which I find it best to read into the verse a little, which as you will see, does not compromise the integrity of the meaning, but it can help with compliance. Again, feel free to use it in your situation if it helps.

One of the things I find that can be very frustrating about marriage is trying to understand how my wife thinks. I have come to realize and accept that I cannot always understand. I am confident that she can definitely justifiably say that she cannot understand my thinking process. Does 1 Peter 3:7 say that I need to understand how she thinks? It does not. What I do understand is that we think differently. So I do not try to think like her or try to figure out what she is thinking. Instead, I try to recall all I know about her and what she will do or say based solely on experience. There is a subtle but reasonable and impactful difference. Where there is history, I try to come to a conclusion based on similar past situations. If there isn't anything to draw from, I no longer burn fuel trying to figure her out. This is one step closer to becoming one. Because we have experienced many different things together and had many conversations, I am pretty sure I can accurately conclude what she will say or do in a given situation. At the very least, I can narrow it down to a couple of choices. It is now easier to line myself up to be in agreement with her.

I used to drive myself to the point of total frustration and anger (another sin) trying to figure out what she was thinking, never being able to do so. That frustration would surface in my conversation with her, ultimately affecting my ability to comply with six of the ten commands we are given as husbands. The moment I shifted to acknowledging that I do not understand how or why she thinks the way she does, everything changed. Now how and why do not matter. No longer do I ask myself, *Does she not see this or that?* I find myself being in a much better position to give honor to her as my wife. I have also come to realize how my way of thinking probably frustrates her. Now, when appropriate, I readily explain my thought process so that she knows there was a reason for my action – it was not just a random act. This easy change facilitates our becoming one. Living with the understanding that I will not always understand – and don't have to – now makes it possible for me to comply with the six commands that I once chased after but were so elusive (like that pot of gold at the end of a rainbow).

Now I am in a much better place to comply with the rest of this command. If I don't get that first part right, the rest is going down in flames.

Men are built differently than women. We must understand that it is our responsibility to protect our wives in every possible manner. Our wives are not children, but in the same way that we protect our children – we need to protect our wives. We must always come to their aid/defense without prejudice. Think – *if someone hurts her, they hurt me. We are one.* Here is another way to look at "weaker vessel" that may help some.

I like to eat at restaurants for many reasons, although I am no longer convinced the meals are worth the price. When we eat out, one of the first things I usually do is cut the meal in half and ask for a to-go container. Usually there are multiple containers to take home (between my wife and me), so I will ask for a bag for the containers. A typical restaurant might have many types of bags. There are bags for the vacuum cleaner. There are larger plastic bags that go into the can in the rest room and there are also large, thick garbage container bags (liners). There is also the thin bag provided for carrying home to-go containers. Technically the server would be correct if he or she returned with any one of these types of bags in hand. However, whenever I ask for a bag, the server always returns with exactly what I was hoping for.

Here is my point: a thin plastic bag with handles was created for a specific purpose – to take home to-go containers. At the same time, a large 55-gallon liner, three mil thick, was also created for a specific purpose. That purpose is very different than our need. Guys, when we look at the phrase "weaker vessel" in the verse above (1 Peter 3:7), we should not at all think of our wives as being deficient or lesser. This mindset will likely fuel negative and incorrect thoughts of superiority. It is this attitude that affects the interaction between man and woman as it often comes across as patronizing or condescending. Like the example with the bag, man and woman were created by God with different purposes. Together they work perfectly for doing all that needs to be done. It is only when the two are used outside of their purpose that things can go awry, as is the case with trying to use a kitchen-sized garbage bag in a 55-gallon trash bin. In this case, the plastic bag made for to-go containers is the "weaker" bag comparatively, but it is the best choice for our need. Conversely, a trash bag liner is not.

By way of another example, I have a very large (sixty ounce), thick, heavy glass mug. It weighs two pounds and fifteen ounces. Yes, I did type that correctly—almost three pounds *empty*. Drinking from it is quite literally a workout made worse once ice is added and a good, strong lemonade is poured into it. That mug works perfectly in that situation. My wife always uses little three-ounce paper cups to rinse her mouth out after brushing her teeth. If my wife were to use my glass mug for that purpose, while the muscular definition in her right forearm might be enviable, it would look ridiculous and be quite cumbersome. At the same time, using her paper cup to hold part of one ice cube and a couple thimblefuls of lemonade would require a visit to at least one mental health professional. Both cups (vessels) were created for specific but different purposes. The paper cup would be the weaker vessel for my needs.

Circling back to our verse, a woman was never made deficient, inferior, or less than. She was wonderfully and perfectly created. However, man and woman were created with different but complementary purposes. To see her as weak because, generally speaking, she cannot hurl a fifty-pound bag of flour over her shoulder and carry it from the car to the pantry doesn't make her weak in a derogatory sense. When we communicate with our wives, we need to do so with understanding, not as if we are more superior. In some situations, she meets a need exactly while we do not. In other situations, we meet a need while she may not. And get this—those situations are not necessarily gender based. If the trash bag and cup examples help you to retrain your brain, do whatever it takes to flip that mindset!

Now for another lesson. Guys, when we find ourselves in a situation in which we need help (and we do need it), be sure that it is not because we think it is beneath us (refer to the glass/bag examples). If you think it is beneath you, she will perceive that, and how do you think that will make her feel? Approach her with those things *only* where "that something in her" makes that thing possible or easier. If we are just nincompoops and cannot do it, admit it. It is an easy thing to do and be sure to let her know she is appreciated. This perspective works wonders as it honors her for the things she can do that only she can do well.

Let me give you a goofy example I am embarrassed to admit. We like to bowl and often bowl in tournaments. I will bowl with different people at different times on different days. It doesn't matter what I try— I cannot keep track of any of it. I don't know why. But, of course, she can and with no effort. She knows this and I know this. In fact, a lot of the other guys do as well. So they will talk to her about my availability. It is not at all beneath me. For some reason I can't. I sometime feel this situation is like Paul's thorn. Never do I make her feel that it is menial. It isn't! This is the perspective I have with everything, and I see them as humbling experiences. I know it's goofy but it's real, and not being able to do many things well seems to buffet me and I am 100-percent okay with that. I don't need to know it all and won't pretend to know it all. But together we do.

It is with these perspectives in mind that we can now go back to the beginning of our verse. Generally speaking, women, pound for pound, are usually weaker than men (emphasizing *generally*). While some men see this as a reason to berate or dominate women, as men of God it should not be ours. Whenever I read this verse I think of being chivalrous. Chivalry originally was put in place to distinguish those in a noble class from the lesser people. Chivalry would later evolve into many things, but to remain true to this topic we will go with the twelfth-century version when chivalry was romanticized (Cartwright 2018). Examples of chivalrous actions that bring honor to women are opening the car door for her, having a server take her order before yours (some women even like when the man orders for her). Chivalry might include pulling out her chair and after she is seated pushing her closer to the table. It could mean running to the car to get an umbrella when at the mall in order to keep her from getting rained on. One directive I did have for my wife from day one: do not touch the trash. I am not compelled to do these things for her because she is "weaker" or incapable. It is out of honor and respect for her. I don't want to touch the trash much less have my wife touch it. That is beneath her! That said, not all women appreciate these actions as some find these acts demeaning. Each of us must find out our wives' position on this type of honor. If she doesn't appreciate it, don't do it. Find other ways to honor her. It could be in speech. It could be in how we dress and carry ourselves when we're together. I should add taking out the trash for her should not be the *only* way we honor her either!

We should also understand this: "Weaker" does not define her capacity for faith, obedience, nor is it a measurement of mental prowess. As men when we get this—we will more readily line ourselves up with the will of God. We will *not* be the guys who lord it over her. Treating her as your perfect complement will not make you less of a man but a much stronger one. You can believe that when the two of you are flowing in his will, everyone else will want in on your "secret" (which really is not a secret at all)!

There are other ways in which we can honor our wives. Some situations dictate that we stand in and "cover" our wives. That can come through intercessory prayer. It is not always necessary that you give advice. I have learned simply to let my wife release pressure she's feeling about one situation or another. Then guess what—I have plenty of ammunition to go to God with when I pray. I don't always have a fix. Sometimes she is not asking for a fix. She knows her situation better and often knows what the fix is but isn't empowered to implement the necessary fix for one reason or another. She just needs to blow off some steam. I have learned to be a pressure release valve. Brother, let me tell you—it is easy and powerful!

Okay, here's another. Have you ever gone somewhere to purchase something but the salesperson speaks only with you and barely acknowledges your wife? For the sake of giving people the benefit of the doubt, I prefer to think it is not out of intentional disrespect but ignorance. This has happened to my wife and me a few times. What do I do? I will divert the conversation to her by asking her for her thoughts. If the setting allows, I might step back so that a defined, isosceles triangle is established. I will not let the salesperson position himself or herself to be directly in front of me only. If after a few of those "bailouts" there's no change in the salesperson's tactics, he or she lost a sale. We will go elsewhere. If I refuse to dishonor her, surely I am not going to let someone else do it!

Another way to show honor is to defend her publicly. Even when we are not in agreement, under no certain terms should others perceive that we are not a unified front. What do you do if she is in the wrong? Doesn't matter. Stand with her. You can always make an adjustment later with "After we had a chance to look this over, *we* are . . ." How is it that Adam ate the fruit when he knew exactly what God said? What about Abraham sleeping with Hagar (Genesis 16)? What about Ananias's and Sapphira's deaths (Acts 5). I believe it is because each of the couples were united, or as Adam refers to it, "one flesh." It was not because the women were nagging, as Delilah did to Samson (leading to his acquiescence and subsequent death—Judges 16). Abdicating your positional responsibility for the sake of appeasement (avoiding confrontation) only postpones the battle and sets up an inevitable war on one or more fronts. Men need to stand firm in what God says and in an understanding and loving way bring her into the truth if she is wrong. Doing contrary will lead to disobedience of God and the possibility of facing his judgement. If she does not give in to do the right thing, don't you give in by doing the wrong thing with her. Pray and stand!

That being said, just because we husbands have been given the responsibility to be the head does not mean we are always right. This is where our exercise in the other precepts/commands (Ephesians 5:25, 28–29; Colossians 3:19) come in to assist. Never should we snub our wives for not agreeing with us. In plain language, that would be the wrong thing to do. Here are two very good reasons to ponder. First, maybe *she* has been given a message from God on what to do (see Luke 1:26–38). How we treat her may very well be a test from God. Will we do the right thing? We do not have to spiritualize it, though. From an everyday, practical standpoint, if she has a greater understanding or more experience in the matter at hand, she can provide insight we do not possess. Wives are with us to complete us, not to compete with us.

That is, unless you are in a head-to-head match at the local bowling alley—her team versus your team. Then all bets are off! After the match, even if you lose, be unified as a couple.

There is one thing I absolutely loathe with every fiber of my being—landscaping. Ugh! I thank God for creating people who love to do the things I truly despise. It is not because I think it is beneath me. I just don't like it at all! As I say that, I will admit that despite my feelings, I am cutting my lawn myself. I have not yet paid someone to cut it for two reasons. First, though I can afford it, I don't hate it enough to let the money go to have it done. Because I do it myself, I can keep the money for what would be *that* bill in my wallet for other things. Second, in my previous experience I was never able to find a lawn care person who considered that someone lives here and wants their lawn to look nice. Instead, when they were done with the cutting, it looked as if they had drawn the short straw with their peers and had to cut it. It never looked like what it did when I cut it myself. So—I cut it myself.

I said all of that hoping that it provides you with context for what I am going to say next. Because I hate to do that one thing, I find it easier to respect what my wife does not like to do. She does not like dealing with the grill at all! With some women there are things they are adamant about not doing. We need to learn to respect those things in the same way we want to be respected for things we do not want to do. My wife knows how much I hate cutting grass, and she has suggested many times that we get someone else to do it. But she knows that when others cut it, it never meets my standards. For all I know, every time I go out to cut the grass she may be saying, "I don't know why he won't get someone else to cut it." She does remind me that I'm not a spring chicken.

Guys, do whatever it takes to get this one right in your mind so that the rest of the commands we are to live by come more easily. Some of you may argue that "weaker" means inferior and less than adequate. I wish you well with this command and all the others. In the end, we need to get it right because whether we get it right or not, we will all be held accountable for what we've done.

V

ENCOURAGEMENT

This section is written with the purpose of encouraging myself and hopefully my fellow brethren in our walk with God (Isaiah 35:3–4; 1 Thessalonians 5:11, 14; Hebrews 3:13). Marriage is a challenging road with so many things coming at us and sometimes coming at us at the same time. But we do not have to take it all on by ourselves. We are all brothers in Christ, and we are all under attack. Situations are coming at us regardless of where we live, how we look, our professions, our language, and so on. Our individual experiences can help each other grow and succeed in this walk. We are all in one of three places at various points in our marriage: coming out of something, at temporary rest, or going into something. Unfortunately, we are usually not given any notice of where we are heading or how long we will be there. This is why we must always be prepared for anything and everything. There are many sources of encouragement available to us, each giving us what we need so we are able to say, "Come what may, I will run this race." To be successful in this race we can rely on the following for help:

1. Prayer and the Holy Spirit
2. Reading, studying, and meditating on his Word
3. Our wives
4. Our own testimonies
5. Encouragement and testimonies from others

There is no better way to find encouragement than to commune with God. David said it this way: "Cast your burden on the Lord, and He shall sustain you; He shall never permit the righteous to be moved" (Psalm 55:22 NASB). When we are walking in his statutes, we can know with confidence that he hears us, that he is concerned about our situation, and that he will act on our behalf though we may never get audible confirmation.

Prayer is a means by which we can take the full load of our burdens, concerns, failures, shame, and such and dump them at the feet of God, releasing us from their weight. God can handle all of them and everyone else's concerns without lifting a finger. He willingly swaps our pain for his comfort. It's like going to coat check at an event and turning in your big, bulky coat for a lightweight ticket. Imagine the Father sitting upon his massive throne, our Savior sitting to his right, waiting for you and me to cast our cares upon him. It is nothing to him, though it may seem insurmountable to us. Unlike coat check, we don't have to go back to him and pick up our cares. I have heard it said too many times to count, "God does not put more on us than we can handle." This is perhaps a bad paraphrase of 1 Corinthians 10:13. I believe the problems of the world *are* more than we can bear. If we could take it all on without him and be successful, we would do that. We try, though! How is he glorified in that?

Make no mistake about it—as men of God, we will face trials. Here is what the Bible says about trials:

- "Consider it all joy, my brethren, when you encounter various trials." (James 1:2 NASB)
- "Blessed is a man who perseveres under trial; for once he has been approved, he will receive the crown of life which the Lord has promised to those who love Him." (James 1:12 NASB)

Consider it all joy? Really? I have faced many trials in my walk with God as I am sure you have. Long ago, before reading and meditating on James 1:2, I would have never described trials as joyous. What was James thinking? When we look at this verse in context, James gives us a clear understanding of why there is joy in trials. He continues—here is where the joy comes in—"knowing that the testing of your faith produces endurance. And let endurance have its perfect result, so that you may be perfect and complete, lacking in nothing" (James 1:3–4 NASB). Knowing that we go through things is so that we can be perfect and complete. The idea of being perfect and complete gives us good reason to be joyful.

What necessitates this call for endurance? The race we are all running has nothing to do with physical strength or speed, but everything to do with remaining firm in Christ. Unlike in the Olympics, we brethren are not competing against each other. We are running together and encouraging each other through it. To endure in this race, one must have considerable patience. In the New Testament alone there are thirty-four occurrences of the word *patience*. It is also one of the characteristics of love (1 Corinthians 13:4). To be more accurate, patience is the first one! Three out of ten God-given directives explicitly use the word *love* (as defined by God). Three of ten isn't too bad, right? But wait—there's more, as they say in almost every infomercial. The remaining seven directives require godly defined love implicitly! Hopefully this will help drive the point home—in order to love our wives (or anyone else) as we are directed to, patience is required. Pulling in what we mentioned earlier, in order to acquire patience, we need to endure trials as patience is its result. If we lack patience, our ability to perform *any one* precept as it pertains to husbandry is not possible. We could never achieve perfect (Job), upright (David), or blameless (Noah) status without patience. Any attempt to circumvent patience is an exercise in futility as it stunts all growth in the Lord. The next time someone is trying our patience, let the person do it—and work through it. That is the only way to grow in all things godly!

Have you ever prayed for patience? I have. If you've never prayed for patience, can you guess what you get when you ask for it? Nope, not patience in a nice, gift-wrapped box, but you will find your request answered through situations in which patience is required. Patience is not given—it is made.

> For everyone who asks receives, and he who seeks finds,
> and to him who knocks it will be opened. Or what man

is there among you who, when his son asks for a loaf,
will give him a stone? (Matthew 7:8–9 NASB)

When we experience trials and tests, know with confidence that
patience is on the way when we work through it. We just need to
persevere so it can be made. That is the only way to get patience—work
it out through situations that require it, much like working out in the
gym. So you say you want more muscle? Okay, let's start with some
dumbbell exercises, and then we will move over to the bench, then
some dips. I encourage you (and me) to count it all joy because God is
answering our prayer.

I hope no one thinks that it seems good not to ask for patience. Ask
or not, we need it for this walk so the situations will inevitably come.
These are the tests and trials of life. I feel that it is better just to ask for
it. Yes, I was the one kid who stood up in class to do my oral speech
first. It wasn't because I liked it. I didn't. It wasn't because I was good
at oral speeches either. I wasn't. I did it solely because since everyone
had to do them, I might as well get it over with. Tests and trials are not
quite a stone when we asked for a loaf, but boy, they can certainly feel
that way sometimes.

What does it mean to persevere? According to Merriam-Webster,
persevere means "to persist in a state, enterprise, or undertaking in spite
of counterinfluences, opposition, or discouragement" (persevere n.d.).
While the Bible does use *persevere* (1 Timothy 4:16), it does uses *endure* (2
Thessalonians 1:4), *established* (Colossians 2:7), *immovable* (1 Corinthians
15:58), *stand* (1 Corinthians 16:13), and *steadfast* (Colossians 1:23). In
other words, in our trials, tests, and tribulations we cannot be shaky,
double-minded, or lukewarm. We cannot cower away from them since
they are essential to our development.

The Bible speaks of the crown of life in only two places: James
1:12 and Revelation 2:10. In both cases it is achieved only by way of
standing firm through trials, tests, and tribulations. I am sure I speak
for at least most of us when I say that we would like to receive the
crown of life.

Last come the verses on testing. I broke up the following scriptures
into three sections because there are different types of testing. Some

testing is acceptable while other types are not. Here is what God's Word says about tests:

- "Behold, I will rain bread from heaven for you; and the people shall go out and gather a day's portion every day, that I may test them, whether or not they will walk in My instruction." (Exodus 16:4 NASB)
- "Do not be afraid; for God has come in order to test you, and in order that the fear of him may remain with you, so that you may not sin." (Exodus 20:20 NASB)
- "The Lord is in His holy temple; the Lord's throne is in heaven; His eyes behold, His eyelids test the sons of men." (Psalm 11:4 NASB)
- "Examine me, O Lord, and try me; Test my mind and my heart." (Psalm 26:2 NASB)

In this first section we see God testing man. Simply put, it is akin to the test we take at the conclusion of training or a course. We are given some information through a training guide and/or lecture; then our memory and recall or comprehension are tested to determine whether we remember and understand the information presented.

We can expect that as we grow in the Word, God is going to test us. Will we put what we know to be true into action or will we do or say things that are contrary? Suffice it to say, failures and successes will be tested repeatedly. It is not one and done. How else will you know that you know you've got it? Unfortunately, if you did not like pop quizzes in school, that is usually all we will ever get. I have never had someone tell me he or she knew what was going to be tested, when it would be tested, or how he or she was going to be tested. For this reason and others, we need to be sure we have solid preachers and teachers. The *only* way to be sure of that is to dig into the Word for ourselves. We must test and verify everything. Hence, the inclusion of book, chapter, and verse throughout this book.

Looking at the Bible's account of the story of Abraham and the sacrifice of his only heir, Isaac, God tested Abraham to see where his heart was. Without question, God already knew he would do just as he asked. This test would be for the benefit of Abraham as well as every believer to follow. If you recall back in "Withholding Is for Taxes," we talked about temptation versus testing. The situation Abraham found himself in was not God leading him to temptation or God tempting him. How are we to process this and have the entire situation line up with all that we know about God? It is quite simple actually. God was testing Abraham's obedience. After all, faith is not faith until it is tested and confirmed. Will he commit his heart to follow God's command? It was not temptation to commit murder.

Looking at this from a relatable standpoint, as fathers we often test the trust of our children. We may stand in the deep end of the pool trying to coax our little ones to jump into our arms. If we break it down, we are essentially testing their faith in us. It is not really for our own benefit (though we will feel good about ourselves once confirmed) but for their benefit. It is from moments like these that the idea of Daddy being a superman forms. Generally speaking, while there might be a hint of trepidation, our kids are willing to jump right in, knowing full well they would sink if we weren't there. Here is another example for those of us without kids, nieces, or nephews but have pets.

I have a staircase that leads downstairs to my basement. Whenever I go down there, my dogs (ten-year-old Shih Tzu siblings) want to follow. One dog will take it upon himself to follow behind me. His sister, on the other hand, will sit at the top of the stairs and bark because under her own power she will not follow. Her brother will walk down under his own power, then sit on the landing between where I am and the top of the stairs where his sister is. She will continue barking until I come get her. It does not matter whether I stand on the landing or two steps down from her—she *will not* trust me and come down the stairs. Hey, wait. I never did anything to facilitate the mistrust either. Needless to say, I *carry* her down.

In this case, as with the pool and my kids, in no way will I let them get hurt. I will be there for them every time. This is similar to the lesson learned from the Abraham, Isaac, and God scenario. God knew he would provide the sacrifice for Abraham. All he had to do, and it came with a lot to lose, was trust that God would take care of the situation somehow. Abraham did and God did. That is where you and I need to be secure. We do our part and trust (test) God and be confident that he will do his part.

Below are more verses but with a different type of testing:

- "Test yourselves to see if you are in the faith; examine yourselves! Or do you not recognize this about yourselves, that Jesus Christ is in you—unless indeed you fail the test?" (2 Corinthians 13:5 NASB)
- "Beloved, do not believe every spirit, but test the spirits to see whether they are from God, because many false prophets have gone out into the world." (1 John 4:1 NASB)
- "I know your deeds and your toil and perseverance, and that you cannot tolerate evil men, and you put to the test those who call themselves apostles, and they are not, and you found them to be false." (Revelation 2:2 NASB)

This group of messages commands testing ourselves and others to be sure speech and action line up with what God says. I remember all throughout my years in school my classmates and me testing each other to make sure we knew all lecture and homework information. On the way home . . .a random question. Bumping into each other in the halls . . . another random question. We would race to be the first person to ask the other a question about the material we learned. This is how we made sure we were always prepared for random quizzes and scheduled tests.

When I was a kid I used to play a game called "I Went on a trip" with my family. That game would begin with the first person saying, "I went on a trip and brought . . ." and then they would tell what they were taking on the trip. The next person would begin their turn by saying, "I went on a trip and brought . . ." whatever the first person brought, then add something of his or her own that he or she would take on the trip. Back and forth things would be recalled and added. Before long there would be a nice little list of items going on vacation! The key to the game was to memorize every item in the right order. Forget something or get the order mixed up—you either lose or get knocked out of the game.

Building your list of to-dos (and do-not-dos) in your walk with God can be done in similar fashion. I recommend starting with the New Testament one command at a time, build a list, and take your time working them out in your life. When a situation relative to a command listed becomes applicable, respond as he commands. Of course, some things may take time to present themselves. For those situations, adding multiple commands is reasonable. Give them some time, *except* those commands that should not require time and meditation like, oh, say . . . the one prohibiting murder!

The difference with testing used in the following verses should be apparent rather quickly:

- "The people quarreled with Moses and said, 'Give us water that we may drink.' And Moses said to them, 'Why do you quarrel with me? Why do you test the Lord?'" (Exodus 17:2 NASB)
- "Surely all the men who have seen My glory and My signs which I performed in Egypt and in the wilderness, yet have put Me to the test these ten times and have not listened to My voice." (Numbers 14:22 NASB)
- "You shall not put the Lord your God to the test, as you tested him at Massah." (Deuteronomy 6:16 NASB)
- "Why do you put God to the test by placing upon the neck of the disciples a yoke which neither our fathers nor we have been able to bear?" (Acts 15:10 NASB)

These verses remind us we must be careful that we never test the Lord. For those who are versed in the word, especially the proponents of tithing, I'm sure you're thinking about the place in God's Word that clearly says, "'Bring the whole tithe into the storehouse, so that there may be food in My house, *and test Me now in this*,' says the Lord of hosts." (Malachi 3:10 NASB, emphasis added).

How do we resolve the seeming conflict between not testing God but then God saying to the Israelites through the prophet Malachi to test him? A simple response might be to test him only in the way that he permits. That would be a fair response, although a bit ambiguous. I would take that a little further by pointing out a very stark difference.

The latest verses involve testing God by crossing his line in order to gauge the severity of the consequences. Or perhaps they don't believe there are any consequences at all. Adolescents use this type of testing quite often.

When God through Malachi says to the Israelites to test him, he was *not* talking about breaking his command then waiting to gauge the strength of his response. He was saying, *Do as I tell you and see how I will bless you for being obedient.* It is in this way that I encourage you, through this book, to test him. Do all that he says to do and see what he does on your behalf. Talk about a blessing we could not contain!

Hopefully you see there is no actual conflict and that there is a clear difference between when it is good and not good to test God. With people there is a limit to the extent of the recourse for violating our wishes. With God there is no limit. Ananias and Sephira, I am confident, would agree with that. Ask King David. Israel would agree with me as well. The problem today is that because God is merciful and long-suffering, believers think they are getting away with something. Only paraphrasing what Jesus told Satan on the pinnacle of the temple— don't test him (Matthew 4:5–7).

This book is the outline of what we are to do. Do what he says. I am confident that whatever response he has for us is immeasurably greater than any and every sacrifice we will ever make as we strive to love our wives as he commands. We already have God's position on that in 1 Samuel 15:22. I encourage myself with this related thought. Sacrifice is good. Obedience is better. Sacrifice along with obedience is best.

As we walk out our individual journeys, it is through our fellowship with other married brothers in Christ that we are to find encouragement. The lone-wolf believer never experiences the benefit of encouragement from others, and it is by no means inconsequential in our walk with God. When God shows up and shows out for others, it reminds us that when we face trials and tribulations, none of which is unique to us, he is there for us just the same. We have confidence in this because with God there is no partiality (Romans 2:11).

A recent study conducted by the Barna Group suggests that married men having a confidant "experience greater relational well-being and satisfaction." It goes on to say that "married practicing Christian with a confidant in their lives are 30 percentage points more likely than those without a confidant to say they are satisfied with their marriage" (Barna:minute Does Having a Confidant Support Men's Relational Well-Being? 2022).

Interestingly, the most apparent problem men often share with me is that they do not have anyone to talk to, no one close enough who can provide valuable insight or at least a well-thought-out opinion. Men's groups are phenomenal when they are grounded in God and are talking about walking out this life with a biblical worldview in an antichrist world. Whenever socialization becomes its purpose, or the gathering is nothing more than a meeting of the He-Man Women-Haters Club (The Little Rascals), it is time to go. It seems apparent that Paul was a witness to the right type of support structure at the church in Thessalonica, hence the encouraging of them to continue in it.

I do not believe that any one person should attempt this walk without some sort of "support structure." Your support structure doesn't need to be anything formal. What is necessary is that the other(s) have a strong biblical worldview in all areas, especially the ones that society bends that Christians are ostracized for because we won't follow suit. One brother needs to be able to say to another, "I understand how you're feeling. It is important and necessary to add to that . . . and this is what God says about that situation. . . ." When we attempt this walk without something like that, it can make the road longer and harder. It is not easy, although possible, to encourage oneself while in a pile of mess.

I spent a large part of my walk without this kind of support structure, and in all honesty, it was not necessarily preferred. It just so happened that most people who were closest to me were not in a place to help for many different reasons. I have prayed for ways I could make myself available to help those walking this walk alone. Taking this journey alone never fails to bring me back to this one verse from the Bible, 1 Peter 5:8: "Be sober, be vigilant; because your adversary the devil walks about like a roaring lion, seeking whom he may devour" (NKJV). Despite our thinking that solitude demonstrates strength, a lone sheep makes for an easier target. There is strength in numbers. Find a good support structure. And just as important, be a good support structure for others.

Last but definitely not least, look to the Scriptures for help. I hear people say that they wish they could hear from God. You can. He speaks to us primarily through his Word. Find Scriptures that give you what you need to keep pressing – they are in there! When you memorize and meditate on them you will be surprised how often they come to mind in time of need. This is yet another reason why I encourage people to read the Bible for themselves. Here are but a few to get you started—

PSALM 1:1–3

How happy is the man who does not follow the advice of the wicked or take the path of sinners or join a group of mockers! Instead, his delight is in the Lord's instruction, and he meditates on it day and night. He is like a tree planted beside streams of water that bears its fruit in season and whose leaf does not wither. Whatever he does prospers. (HCSB)

It is important to read the verses of Psalm 1:1–3 and all the others noted in this book prayerfully and studiously. Sometimes initial reading may seem to say one thing, but upon further study, and clarity through prayer, we see another way of looking at it. At first glance it may seem that all one needs to do is enjoy a sermon, Bible study, or Sunday school lesson. It may look as though if we avoid *some* of the wicked, *some* of the sinners, and avoid joining groups of mockers, we will be like the tree described, and all that we put our hands on will prosper. That is not the message we should glean from these verses. How can I say this with such certainty? Because that is not what these verses say.

If you are not familiar with Psalm 1, I encourage you to read it. It is short and sweet, but it is bursting at the seams with so much information. Reading it creates a beautiful picture in my mind for his faithful followers. Psalm 1 solidifies any argument between those who believe our reward comes in the hereafter and those who believe our reward is available now. The rewards are available in both.

I have heard too many times to count how Jesus "hung out with" sinners. Well, yeah, but it was not for the purposes of playing Pictionary, Poker, or pickleball. Others may argue that if we separate ourselves from others, how can we be that light on the hill? We should understand that a hill by its very definition is higher than the valley where the mess is! The problem is that we want to keep company with those who will drain our light of its intensity, to the point at which the light is no longer. The only difference between "the believer" and the rest is that the believer goes to church on Sunday and may even hold a position, sadly and to the detriment of the believer (not the non-Christian). This subject is worthy of a book of its own and is a bit off the grid as it relates to this one.

Reeling it in, though, along the same vein, I am aware of many different attitudes when it comes to obedience to our God's commands. On opposite ends of the band are those who follow Christ's commands as their personal form of worship and devotion, and those who use salvation as an "eternal-life insurance policy." The rest is made up of those who ping-pong between the two, based on their current circumstance. The first psalm, along with many other verses throughout the Bible, keeps me encouraged as I live out a life of worship and devotion. It says there is happiness in not following the advice of the wicked, walking in the path of sinners, or joining in with a bunch of mockers ("scornful" in the KJV). Job referred to his friends as "scornful" and we know how much they put Job through, so much so that God was going to "deal with them" were it not for their sacrifice and Job's intercessory prayer (Job 42:7–9).

Notice in these verses that this person delights in God's instruction. Knowing and following his commands is a delight. As mentioned earlier, his perspective is not that God's instruction is restrictive but that it is freeing. The current cultural climate is one that does not appreciate being told what to do, how to live, or what to say or not say. It wants complete autonomy and self-governance, or "What works for you may not work for me, and that's fine as long as you don't encroach on my rights."

Rules are in place with good reason. God has set before us in his Word and in our hearts how we are to live. First, knowing they are there brings me great joy. Second, living by them gives me great pleasure because I know with confidence that the fullness in this life comes only by way of living by them.

Have you ever studied Joshua's story? Here is the highly paraphrased version: God has Israel at a place right before going into the promised land. He directs Moses to send twelve spies, one from each tribe, to preview the land of Canaan. After forty days the spies return with their report. They all report that the land is good, but ten report their fear of fighting against its existing inhabitants. However, Caleb and Joshua have a different report:

> The land which we passed through to spy out is an exceedingly good land. If the Lord is pleased with us, then He will bring us into this land and give it to us—a land which flows with milk and honey. Only do not rebel against the Lord; and do not fear the people of the land, for they will be our prey. Their protection has been removed from them, and the Lord is with us; do not fear them. (Numbers 14:7–9 NASB)

Although all the people were against the two to the point of stoning them both, they were secured in who God is and what he had said to them. Because of their disbelief, the Lord planned to wipe them all out by way of a larger and stronger nation. But Moses interceded on their behalf. Instead of a violent death, only Joshua, Caleb, and those younger than twenty years would see his promise. The rest would die having never stepped foot in the promised land. More time was wasted in the wilderness as they waited for the adults to die off. Eventually they went in and possessed the land, entirely trusting God to fight for and deliver them against overwhelming odds.

How does any of this information help us in our marriages? If God says that he gives us favor, then we need to have confidence in that, regardless of how things appear. If he says we have found a good thing, we found a good thing. Let no one convince us of anything contrary. We want to live out his promise, not die before we ever see it come to fruition in our lives. We need to have Joshua and Caleb's attitude as it relates to our marriages and everything else: "I may be going through some stuff right now, but you said it's good, that I have your favor, and that's good enough for me." Keep pressing and hoping. This life is not solely about living for the afterlife. The end of verse 3 explicitly tells us—when we steer clear of evildoers, take joy in the law of the Lord and meditate on it without ceasing. Whatever we set out to do will be successful. We must see there being no other option but success for our marriages, provided that we live up to our end of related promises.

The Bible tells us that the enemy's goals are to steal, kill, and destroy. He cannot fight against the reality of Psalm 1 (or any other promise). Whatever God says will happen, will happen. The enemy knows this, but knowing will not stop him from striving to accomplish his goals. There are no rules of engagement as far as he is concerned. He will attack any and everything leading up to God's promise taking effect. If everything we do *will* prosper, the enemy will go after everything we must do before that. How can he use our friends and family to his benefit? Is it possible to convince us that God's law is too restrictive? What distractions can he use to keep us from meditating on God's instruction? Sports? TV? It doesn't matter. I have seen him use church commitments to distract believers. The result? The tree will not be planted beside an abundant supply of water. Because of that, its leaves will be withered, prosperities thwarted. Today there is such a push on the message of the grace of God and very little (at best) on obedience. New believers must wonder, *Are there any rules to this life at all?* We as genuine believers know that joyful obedience is paramount to prospering.

Men, as with the topic of this book, marriage, and everything else, I encourage us all to seek the will of God. He makes it knowable, but it is not simply handed to us. We must go get it. There is some effort involved on our part. One of my favorite quotes that started me in my journey of study is by Rev. Arthur W. Pink: "The Bible does not yield its meanings to lazy people." While I am not calling anyone lazy, the point is that it takes effort. This is where so much of Christendom fails. Do not believe for one second that all that's needed is our attendance in church services on Sundays. And this walk with God is far more than our volunteerism effort. Be the tree in Psalm 1. Be happy as that man is said to be. Be prosperous in all you do, which includes your marriage and walk with God. You were made for this!

ISAIAH 40:28–31

Have you not known? Have you not heard? The everlasting God, the Lord, The Creator of the ends of the earth, Neither faints nor is weary. His understanding is unsearchable. He gives power to the weak, And to those who have no might He increases strength. Even the youths shall faint and be weary, And the young men shall utterly fall, But those who wait on the Lord Shall renew their strength; They shall mount up with wings like eagles, They shall run and not be weary, They shall walk and not faint. (NKJV)

I sometimes wonder—Is God as tired of hearing my petitions as I am of hearing myself repeat them? I know he isn't, but I am sincere when I say that thought does come to mind. Sometimes I think, *He's heard this before from earlier prayers—there's no sense asking this one more time.* But when I think of this verse, it reminds me first that while I may grow weary, though I shouldn't, God does not. He doesn't tire of hearing my petitions. He already knows what I need before I even ask. Furthermore, he doesn't grow weary of showing himself strong in every situation I find myself in. But it is in his timing, not mine.

Earlier we went over God's expectations of us in how we need to relate to our wives in an understanding way. When he says, "Fear not," he says it because he understands why we may have reason to feel fear. When he leaves us a means of escape from temptation, it is because he understands temptation and our weakness. He understands disappointment, hunger, anger, and sadness. He relates to our problems, although unlike us, his understanding knows no beginning or end. We need to realize that what he asks from us he also uses with us. Though our understanding is limited, we need to relate to our wives as he does with us, and we do not need his level of understanding to fully comply. His commands are reasonable.

Whenever we feel like giving up on anything, not only our marriages, he can give us power. His power will increase our strength, that we may soar as eagles and run without tiring. We need only ask with expectancy. Continue to hope in him—as his hope does not disappoint.

MATTHEW 11:12

From the days of John the Baptist until now the kingdom of heaven suffers violence, and the violent take it by force. (NKJV)

Admittedly, to this day Matthew 11:12 continues to be a tough one for me. As far back as I can remember, my parents always taught me (and reminded me when necessary) to be polite. Whenever I would ask for something, they would say, "And what do you say?" I would then respond, "Please." Then when the item was given to me—"*Now* what do you say?" I would then spout, "Thank you." Then I would receive all sorts of accolades. I can also remember back to many of my younger days, after those polite responses had became rote, many adults saying that I was so polite or that I had such good manners. Boy, did I love hearing those words! To this day I hear the same message with other little people here and there: "Oh, they're so polite! Such good kids!" Yes, I am guilty of using that today with young people. Don't get me wrong—this is a great thing!

Here's the rub. Some promises of God we can actually "demand." Boy, does that make me uneasy, as I am sure some of you are. In prayer I feel that I am literally on my knees before the throne speaking with God. In no way, shape, or form do I feel comfortable with making demands. Yet Christ said to! Whenever I pray the Lord's Prayer it seems as if the hair on my neck stands at attention when I get to the lines "Give us this day . . ." "Forgive us our debts . . ." "Lead us not into . . ." and "Deliver us from . . ." I mean, who am I to tell the creator and sustainer of all things what to do? Comparatively, I am nobody. I am nothing.

I have never had the pleasure of walking about this planet with any sense of entitlement. I was raised to be polite and respectful, and perhaps that is a consequence of a bygone era. I know I am a joint heir with Christ (Romans 8:17). I know that I should go boldly before the throne (Hebrews 14:16), but it is nevertheless a conscious effort to put into practice. Apparently I am not the only one as I hear others pray publicly. Here is the truth: we do not need to pray asking for things God has already promised us. Looking at the Lord's Prayer more closely, we can see that every one of those demands is attached to a promise.

"Give us this day our daily bread."

> For this reason I say to you, do not be worried about your life, as to what you will eat or what you will drink; nor for your body, as to what you will put on. Is not life more than food, and the body more than clothing? . . . But if God so clothes the grass of the field, which is alive today and tomorrow is thrown into the furnace, will He not much more clothe you? You of little faith! Do not worry then, saying, 'What will we eat?' or 'What will we drink?' or 'What will we wear for clothing?'" (Matthew 6:25, 30–31 NASB)

"And forgive us our debts"

In 1 John 1:9 we find the promise "If we confess our sins, he is faithful and righteous to forgive us our sins and to cleanse us from all unrighteousness" (NASB). Here we are again with another conditional statement. The hypothesis for testing is the confession of our sins; the conclusion is that he will forgive us and cleanse us. This should not be taken to mean that we need to go before a priest and confess our sins. There is only one capable of forgiving sin and that is God. Confessing and apologizing to the offended is a godly principle (James 5:16).

"And do not lead us into temptation, But deliver us . . ."

For this we need to go to James 1:13–16 (examined previously):

> Let no one say when he is tempted, "I am being tempted by God"; for God cannot be tempted by evil, and He Himself does not tempt anyone. But each one is tempted when he is carried away and enticed by his own lust. Then when lust has conceived, it gives birth to sin; and

when sin is accomplished, it brings forth death. Do not be deceived, my beloved brethren. (NASB)

This one is more straightforward than the others. There is no condition to be met. It is just stated fact. Whenever you feel tempted to do something wrong, it is *not* from God. It is our flesh or that of the enemy trying to capitalize on our desires. This is akin to the temptation of Jesus after having been baptized by John. While Jesus was in the wilderness Satan showed up and tried to tempt him on three separate occasions. We know that Jesus rejected all of them with the Word. As with Jesus, so it should be with us. Whenever we find ourselves at a place of temptation, we can fall back on this. God provides us with an escape hatch, that we might get out quickly and easily. Paul says in his first letter to the church at Corinth,

> No temptation has overtaken you but such as is common to man; and God is faithful, who will not allow you to be tempted beyond what you are able, but with the temptation will provide the way of escape also, so that you will be able to endure it. (1 Corinthians 10:13 NASB)

From a personal standpoint I have found that in my life, whenever I didn't take the first out, there were other "escape hatches" before the commission of sin. Said differently, it is my experience that whenever I committed a sinful act, repeated deliberate disregard was always observable in hindsight. The longer I entertained conversation with my flesh (another enemy of mine), the deeper the descent. But on the way down there were glaring opportunities to get out of the situation. God was so good even in my defiance.

Jesus is telling us in his model prayer there is no need to ask for these things. In fact, we are not demanding these things (I need to remind myself of this). This prayer is for our own sake. It is a reminder. We do our part – God will do his.

Going full circle, we come back to our opening, encouraging verse, Matthew 11:12. We need to understand that we are in fact taking what

God has fully offered to us. A purposed and determined mindset is needed in order to get what God has promised. We cannot get those things by being passive. We cannot just sit around asking and pleading. We must go get them. That means living up to our end of the bargain, where it pertains, and it looks something like this: *God, you said in your Word that* [enter promise here]. *I have been and continue to operate within the boundaries you have set. Because of that, I can rest confidently knowing that you've already taken care of it and that I need only to wait for it to come to fruition.*

This is where patience has its perfect work (James 1:4–8). I hope it is obvious that there are definitely those things that we do need to ask for. It is just that in this case, asking is not a prerequisite of receiving his promises.

Here it is in a nutshell: Know what his promises are as they pertain to your situation, know what it is that you must do, *do it*, and then wait patiently reminding yourself of what he is going to do until it is received. You must keep living up to your end of the bargain, though. Don't try to walk in obedience today, claim the promise, and then have your way the rest of the time. This is not a one and done. Go get what God has for you.

We will be going through more promises in this section. Some are innate to his character. Others require our participation. Pay close attention to both.

MARK 10:27

Jesus looked at them and said, "With men it is impossible, but not with God; for with God all things are possible." (NKJV)

Mark 10:27 is a gold nugget and provides me with so much encouragement in so many different situations that you can easily say it is my go-to verse. This verse most definitely brings the peace of Christ to the mildest of issues all the way up to those that seem insurmountable. I have had friends believe their wives no longer wanted to be married to them—but they have not left. There is no need wasting mental energy on "What if she leaves?" Think instead on this verse and what will you need to do not to get into this situation again!

I should say that because of free will, God will not make anyone love another. He doesn't even force us to love *him*. What I do believe is that God will bring about situations in which the qualities in us that she needs or misses can be seen again, those things that no one else is quite capable of, softening her heart for us. God can turn *any* situation around. This is the message to share with your fellow brother. This is the message to carry through your storm.

Who says a leopard cannot change its spots? How about an old dog learning new tricks? With God a camel can fit through the eye of a needle! Our situations are not impossible or even difficult for him. We as brothers just need to stand firm in our faith in him. God alone is all-powerful, having complete sovereignty. Instead of thinking the bad side of "What if?"—hope only on the good side. What if in the next five minutes this thing turns around? What will you do differently? What will you say differently? It is that kind of faith that moves mountains. I implore you to just believe.

All of us reading this book are in different places for different reasons. Some brothers are saying, "Boy, I need to make a lot of changes in myself!" Others are thinking, *There is no way I can do this without her making changes.* Get away from those negative thoughts! This is one of the ways in which we need to be renewing our minds (Romans 12:2). This renewing may not take place overnight, but you have to believe that with God's help it will happen. Otherwise, what is the point in any of this? If you are in a place of wanting to give up, that was rhetorical!

JOHN 16:33

I have told you these things, so that in me you may have peace. In this world you will have trouble. But take heart! I have overcome the world. (NIV)

It has become all too familiar. Give your life to Christ and receive all of his blessing. Bless this. Bless that. But this perspective, if it is the only perspective, could not be farther from the truth. From our very own Savior we know that there will be trouble in this world, and that was a message not just for the twelve but also for all his disciples to come. There are too many verses in the Bible that prove this to be true. If we are being warned that there is an enemy out there whose purpose is to bring trouble, why do we buy into this lie? There is a very easy answer, although somewhat unsettling. I am going to take the long way because I do not want to lead anyone to my conclusion. I will present my case. If you agree, good. If you do not agree, that is fine too. Nevertheless, what Jesus says in this verse still remains true. To start, we will look at only one example of the trouble that comes and just how soon it begins—through the parable of the sower:

> That same day Jesus went out of the house and sat by the lake. Such large crowds gathered around him that he got into a boat and sat in it, while all the people stood on the shore. Then he told them many things in parables, saying: "A farmer went out to sow his seed. As he was scattering the seed, some fell along the path, and the birds came and ate it up. Some fell on rocky places, where it did not have much soil. It sprang up quickly, because the soil was shallow. But when the sun came up, the plants were scorched, and they withered because they had no root. Other seed fell among thorns, which grew up and choked the plants. Still other seed fell on good soil, where it produced a crop—a hundred, sixty or thirty times what was sown. Whoever has ears, let them hear. (Matthew 13:1–9 NIV)

I would like to draw your attention to a few salient points, only briefly as anything more involved would be outside the scope of this book. Jesus provides his disciples (and us) with the meaning of this parable, and it is found in verses 18–23:

- Key #1: Scattered seed represents the message about the kingdom (the gospel).

- Key #2—Rocky ground is someone who hears the message of the kingdom and loves it, but when *trouble and persecution* show up they quickly fall away.
- Key #3—Certain seed falls among thorns, which happens when the message is heard *but the worries of life and lies about wealth choke the message*, making it meaningless in the hearer's life.

Observe two things. First, trouble and persecution show up at the scene immediately. The message is heard and received with great joy. I am not sure if you've ever witnessed a Billy Graham crusade, but I will tell you if you have not that it is amazing to see just how the move of God was so strong. Borrowing a word from the Bible, "throngs" of people would desire to be converted as a result of hearing the gospel message. I have to emphasize—*huge* numbers of people came forward, all wanting to come to Christ, not to mention the huge numbers of people there who were already believers. Anyway, here is my point: Jesus's description of rocky ground and smothering thorns would happen to many of them. The truth is many of us who are active in church will see the same thing happen to new believers. "Life" hits them, and then they fall away or just never walk in the fullness that salvation brings.

Here it is, and we spoke about this before—the enemy's objective is to keep us from the message of salvation. If he cannot, he will try everything to make it ineffective in our lives. This attack, which makes up the rocky ground, comes immediately. But just like weeds and thorns in our yards (arrgh!), they sprout up at random times and places.

In our current day everyone seems to be anxious about so many different things: the U.S. political scene, retirement, the environment, taxes, immigration, violence, selfishness, healthcare, rudeness, the new generation, the job market, inflation, corporate greed and insensitivity, Social Security, food shortages, and on and on. All of this just makes me anchor in and be sure my seatbelt is on and properly worn. At some point the Father is going to tell his Son to get his bride. I need to be sure I am ready with oil in my lamp. I know the enemy is using all of this that the briars and thorns might suppress the gospel from manifesting in my life. I never lose sight of that.

If we know this is true and we do know that it is, why aren't all believers (babes in Christ and veterans alike) warned at conversion and reminded more often? Why has the gospel message become so diluted? Many churches are nothing more than buildings with revolving doors. While some are walking in, others are walking out. It is as if the church has a maximum occupancy rating. When the number of people reaches the capacity, no one is allowed in until someone leaves. Remember shortly after the onset of COVID-19 how only a certain number of people were allowed to shop in a store at a given time? It seems like that is what's going on in many churches. How sad a state we are living in!

I hope the message of this book is clear and not sugar-coated—we are at war, and as in all wars, it is not pretty. There are casualties on both sides. Men, I want you to fight for God's truth in your marriage. I want you to stand firm knowing God is with you, and he is most certainly looking for fighters like you and me. This book is a recruitment of fighters. I am looking for you too! I believe beyond a shadow of doubt that God stirred me up to stir others up. In the very same way, he has stirred up others in all the other areas in life. Some are focused on finances. Some are focused on children. Others are focused on prayer. The list goes on and on. You and I are a standard he is raising up against the enemy.

Jesus says we would face problems. But he leaves us with what should be incredibly comforting words—we need not worry about those problems. He has overcome the world. Because he has overcome the world, we know that being in him, we are also overcomers. But being overcomers in no way implies that this walk is some sort of stroll through the park. Far from it.

Do not let the enemy steal the gospel message from you. Remember that its message is not limited to the topic of salvation but covers all of its promises, including the favor God has given you because you are married. Salvation is free, but almost all of the rest of the promises we have to go and get (largely through the testing of our faith, patience, and perseverance). He's told you all these things—why? That you may have peace. Peace does not mean things will not happen. That would contradict his very next statement. Peace is calm regardless of circumstances.

As I close out my comments about this encouraging verse, please consider something: If this message is preached to all believers – the truth about what is to come – do you think that it would help build stronger disciples? Or do you think the cost of "scaring off" new converts is greater? Permit me to ask another question: Does Jesus give the command to bring in new converts or make disciples? Imagine how strong the church would be if the Word that was delivered came with the thorn-killing message it should! While that is not meant to blame anyone for anything, it is the reality that we find our church in. Too often the blessings of God are delivered with such passion and enthusiasm but very little to nothing on living the way God expects us to and the consequences of not doing so.

I am here to tell you that the enemy will come after anything and everything. Yes, even our marriages. Rephrase—especially marriages, and that amounts to attacks on husband, wife, or both. It has been proven true generation after generation that everything in society will consequently suffer. It is akin to destroying the root of a tree. With damaged or dead roots, everything above them will suffer and die. Why would the enemy waste time and energy cutting off individual leaves up in the canopy of a tree?

ROMANS 8:28–29

> We know that all things work together for good to those
> who love God, to those who are the called according to
> His purpose. For whom He foreknew, He also predestined
> to be conformed to the image of His Son, that He might
> be the firstborn among many brethren. (NKJV)

Many Christians love to partially quote Romans 8:28. I'm not sure if it's for sake of brevity or if they truly have no idea of what the rest of the verse and the following one say and imply. We are going beyond the words "for good" in an effort to see what this promise entails:

- "to those who love God"—Jesus says that obedience is a demonstration of love for him. To him, love does not equate to our casual use of the word.

- "the called according to His purpose"—What is his purpose? Paraphrasing for brevity here, it is to demonstrate his manifold wisdom to the powers, principalities, and rulers of darkness through the church (Ephesians 3:10).
- "conformed to the image of His son"—See also 2 Corinthians 3:18 and Colossians 3:10.

After reading all that is contained in this book, I hope that it stands out that our roles as husbands are a type of relationship that Jesus has with the church. As we move away from being self-centered to living the commands of God, we will look more like Christ. Every time we walk out his commands, we demonstrate just how wonderfully and magnificently brilliant our God is to the demonic world. They have power to influence our walk from a realm we cannot see. Yet we choose to obey God despite the obstacles. The devil and his cohorts had no idea that killing Jesus would give us the power to reconnect with God. As such, we are able to use that power to overcome evil, such as adultery, mistreating our wives, and not working out the responsibilities we have in our homes and community. It is by our consistently meeting those conditions that we can be confident that all things will work out for our good.

Remember—our good may not always align with what we would like. By way of example, we may want a new job but it never comes to us. It could be that God has something for us to do where we are, and until that is accomplished, we cannot leave. There could be any number of reasons for us to remain where we are. Here is where we can place our confidence. When we get to a place where there are two or many choices and none of them matter because all of them will work out for our good, we are in a place of peace of mind, rest, joy, and such. When I say "none of them matter" I am not at all suggesting a place where we no longer care.

Regarding the real world, not caring what our wives do because they won't listen *is not* the message I am trying to convey. That stance could not be any farther away from what I am suggesting. I am not talking about a place of giving up but rather totally giving in to the will of God, having complete trust in him because of what he's said. Turning that situation on its head, because we have confidence in God's promises and we are walking accordingly, we can stand firm where we are, knowing that God will show up. While we don't have to worry, we can pray. We must continue doing all that God expects of us, knowing that whatever he does will be for our good. The challenge is patience, of course, but also not boxing God in, which will likely be very difficult at first. We want to give God our recommendations. This is not trust but rather, and I apologize for saying it, "baby-Christian" thinking. It may work early in our walk with God, but as we mature we need to get to a place where we trust him: *God, I have no idea what you are going to do, but I know whatever you do will be for my good.* When we let God be God and not tell him what we want done, he shows up in a way that can be accounted only to him. I call this a blessing with the fingerprint of God on it.

But what does "according to his purpose" mean? That is a stipulation on this promise. Here is an excerpt of a letter Paul wrote to the church in Ephesus that speaks of God's eternal purpose:

> . . . to make plain to everyone the administration of this mystery, which for ages past was kept hidden in God, who created all things. His intent was that now, through the church, the manifold wisdom of God should be made known to the rulers and authorities in the heavenly realms, according to his eternal purpose that he accomplished in Christ Jesus our Lord. In him and through faith in him we may approach God with freedom and confidence. I ask you, therefore, not to be discouraged because of my sufferings for you, which are your glory. (Ephesians 3:9–13 NIV)

I believe this means that what we do by faith shows the manifold wisdom of God to the rulers and authorities in the heavenly realm. These are the same beings spoken of in Ephesians 6:12. Here is why I believe that: While Paul speaks specifically of his eternal purpose being accomplished in Jesus by the cross, *everything* we are able to do by extension is because of the work of Christ on the cross. It's like the Russian Matryoshka doll. Christ's work at the cross is the largest accomplished purpose that encapsulates our purpose. When "we" heal the sick, it is made possible only through the cross and that being only one manifestation of the manifold wisdom of God. When we stand firm against the temptation of the enemy, it is another manifestation of the manifold wisdom of God, and it is made possible only because of the cross. When we convince other young men to live right and for God, it is a manifestation of the manifold wisdom of God, and it is made possible only through the cross. Every one of these works is done by his purpose as part of the church. All of them demonstrate just how brilliant God's plan of atonement is. While the list is endless, I do want to make the point that walking out our purpose as married men of God to our wives is yet another manifestation of the manifold wisdom of God, made possible only through Jesus and the cross. This work is not to be taken lightly. We must go out and show his wisdom to the powers and principalities and rulers of the air.

I am confident if the enemy had any idea of the power of the cross, he would have offered his own angels to guard him in all his ways. If possible, *they* would have held him up with their own hands so that his foot would not strike a stone.

My hope is that as men, we will find confidence in living out our purpose and that our purpose is part of a much larger purpose, God's eternal purpose. My hope is that as men, we find confidence in knowing that *every* act of obedience shows God's enemies just how boundlessly brilliant our God is, and the cross is just one tiny microcosm (but infinitely significant) of the unfathomable wisdom of our God. We must do all we can to show every spirit of darkness just how magnificent the plan and execution of the cross is through our daily walk in him. No promise, nothing we do, is possible without Jesus and *that* cross! Thank you, Jesus!

1 CORINTHIANS 15:58

> My beloved brethren, be steadfast, immovable, always abounding in the work of the Lord, knowing that your labor is not in vain in the Lord. (NKJV)

First Corinthians 15:58 is another one of my favorites! The task before us as married men is without question the work of the Lord. Remember:

while it may take days, weeks, months, or even years of sowing before the harvest comes in, know that God most definitely notices our work. Galatians 6:9 comes immediately to mind: "Let us not lose heart in doing good, for in due time we will reap if we do not grow weary" (NASB). While "due time" is a relative term, we must be faithful because we know for sure he is. His "due time" may not be as soon as ours, but the harvest will arrive right on time.

You should be fully prepared to face difficulties in this walk with God. Some of it will come from within (our flesh) and some will come from without (spiritual forces and those being used by the enemy). Despite these tough battles and ongoing wars, it does get easier. Our flesh is like the wild horse a cowboy tries to tame in movies. Yes, it bucks and snorts and kicks and snorts more, but after several minutes the horse is under the cowboy's control. Before the episode is over, the horse has a saddle and two pairs of iron shoes, and it is being ridden like a show pony. If only it were that easy.

For some, taming the flesh is more like a rodeo where we are the bull-rider. In this, though, there is no eight-second limit and no clowns to distract the bull as we get our bearings should we fall off. The purpose of our holding on is to break our bull so that we can put a bit in its mouth and steer it where we want to go. Imagine that! Despite the spinning, kicking, bucking, and snorting, we need to get that bull under our control. We cannot be discouraged by the spills and knocks taken. If we are persistent, it will eventually come under our control.

We must stand by what we know the Word of God says and never waver from it. Without question, situations are going to present themselves in which we have a chance to do something that isn't right. Sometimes right and wrong are obvious. Other times there is the uneasiness in the gut we need to pay attention to. I have learned not to go against the gut, and I am convinced that we have it for more than digestive purposes. Despite the things we give up because the Word or the gut says to, we need to be prepared for sacrifices. Obedience to God will always prove worth every effort taken. Sometimes the results can bring us to a place where we say we would have sacrificed more and sooner if we knew the outcome would be so great. Stand firm in doing what is right by your wife regardless of the sacrifice. He sees it all and will reward you for diligent obedience. When you do right by her, you are actually doing right by God. Never lose sight of that.

COLOSSIANS 3:23–24

Whatever you do, work at it with all your heart, as working for the Lord, not for human masters, since you know that you will receive an inheritance from the Lord as a reward. It is the Lord Christ you are serving. (NKJV)

There is no explanation needed for Colossians 3:23–24 because these verses are clear and straightforward—not much room for misinterpretation. Nevertheless, I will say this much— This assignment of being a godly husband should not be looked upon with disdain, regret, or apathy. The assignment could not be more of a stark contrast. As we walk out our assignment as husbands, we should look forward to every day because every day potentially has something for us whether it is growth, reward, a greater bond with our wives, or hearing directly from God. He is interested in everything we do, and we should give this assignment everything we have and with all that he adds to us.

Unlike working for our earthly bosses, with God our value is never taken for granted. With God we don't wait until the end of the year to be rewarded for doing what we are asked to do. He rewards us more often than we probably realize. Our God is patient and is not looking for any reason to write us up. He hired us when we weren't even qualified for the position. Without him we wouldn't be able to do the job. He pours into us all we need that we might be successful. He loves us and trusts us. He doesn't look over our shoulders for our failures. He looks to see where he can build us up. He truly has an open-door policy. He never asks us to do more with less.

We have a job working for the absolute greatest master who ever was or ever will be. He loves us more than anyone else ever could or better than anyone else would if he or she could. He wants us to be successful men of God, so much so that he willingly gives us all we will ever need for our journey. It's when we truly realize just those things that we really begin our journey toward truly loving him as he desires. That is when the work we do for him and in his name gives us pleasure. Regardless of how small or large the task is, we would give it all we have.

We have an assignment, though it may not be a glamorous one. I don't mean it to sound as if we are doing something that belongs on Mike Rowe's *Dirty Jobs*. Being the husband God calls us to be for our wives definitely is not. But being a good husband won't make us loads of money or give us prestige. Here on earth there is no fame or fortune promised with being a godly husband. But to God it is vitally important. These verses from Paul let us know that with the right disposition there is great reward, an inheritance. This is from the only God, who has unlimited access to everything valuable and desirable, the God who created everything we deem valuable and to whom everything belongs. He can create anything out of nothing. If there are more precious minerals scattered about the heavens on other planets in other galaxies, he put them there! This is the resource we have access to that the world does not. While they cannot take their wealth with them, we build wealth both here and in the hereafter. While I don't intend to sound materialistic, it is Paul reminding us of what is available to us. If it is incentive that you need, Paul gave it to us here. All that we can collectively imagine is far less than what God has available to us.

We work hard on our jobs to get a bonus check. We work hard now that we might retire comfortably earlier. We work hard now so that our kids can go to college and get a good head start in life. We need to give him our all. And when we give him our all, it has to be nothing short of our best. While *all* is a quantitative measure, our best is *qualitative*. He deserves both. He is our God, the one and only true, living God.

WRAPPING THINGS UP

Well, gentlemen we made it through to the end of this discourse. Thank you for sticking around. As mentioned at the outset of this book and throughout, walking with God as it pertains to marriage is challenging, although it was never intended to be that way. What makes the walk challenging is our fallen condition. Our flesh (inclinations and thoughts) is in opposition to the law of God. It takes a conscious and concerted effort to exchange our ways for his ways and our thoughts for his thoughts. Nevertheless it is possible, and regardless of the challenge, he expects us to live by his way. As it is with our physical lives here on this earth, our spiritual lives come with costs and rewards. The good news is that we do not have to wait until the life after to experience some of the rewards. We must always remember—*his ordinances are not suggestions, and they are not set before us that we might fail.*

I am sure you caught this already, but did you notice that marriage standards of the world are in complete opposition to God's – marriage's creator? Interdependence is an essential element in a Godly marriage. Merriam-Webster's defines interdependence as dependent upon one another and mutually dependent. We've looked at creation and marriage throughout this text. Marriage as designed by God necessitates mutual dependency for it to function as God intended. Husbands need the help of wives and wives need the help of husbands. They were not created with identical natures. If our wives are not onboard with this, the journey will likely be extremely challenging. Challenging or not we must not forget we are accountable for *only* what we do. Making the journey more difficult is the squawking of others in our ears. If the missus is not living a life devoted to pleasing God, our interdependence will reek of codependence to the world. This is going to be repulsive to many, but here is a reminder—priority number one is your vertical relationship with God. Secondarily, our horizontal relationship with our wives. What others have to say isn't ranked at all. When she treats us as she desires we must not respond in kind but with love. We will find favor, answers to our prayers, blessings, and reward in heaven for our obedience and sacrifice. Fight the good fight!

★ ★ ★

When I was in basic training at Lackland Air Force Base in Bexar County, Texas, many years ago, I will admit that the first night was terrifying! The first week was brutal. The mental stress was through the roof (fellow military members in the corps, navy, and army, feel free to insert your jokes here). The yelling, the barrage of insults—everything was just rough. But it was not until my second week of training that it came to me: The training instructors (TIs) are not going through all of this because they *want* to send me home. Too much time and money were invested to get me here just to send me back. They are up to something else—something greater than what I see and feel. Mind you, I did absolutely zero research about basic training or the military before going in. Neither did I personally know anyone who went into any branch of service. But it was not until that moment that basic training began to be so much easier (fellow military from the other branches insert more jokes here).

I believe this walk with God is similar to my military experience to a small degree. He didn't put these things in place because he wants me to revert to the old me and the old life—working for the enemy. Instead, there are things about me that need to be worked out because those things are contrary to the character and life God desires for me. When I came to that knowledge, that is when everything changed. I have all confidence that God gave me that experience in the military so I could draw on it later in my walk with him.

166

As I sit here thinking through my concluding words, I cannot help wondering if you are thinking that I should have included our wives' responsibilities. After all, as the saying goes, "It takes two to tango." My initial response is to say something you may not hear often enough: "You're right!" It does take two committed people to make a marriage work. As I mentioned earlier, I struggled with which path to take. But I prayed about it, and I am ready to respond. Sorry—I ran out of room!

With all seriousness, I do not believe adding the wife's responsibilities would be expedient for any of us. I have studied the wife's responsibilities almost as rigorously as I did for husbands. Knowing what I know about their duties has not always proven to be useful to me in my walk with God. In fact, I found that knowing them often times became a stumbling block. Looking at what she should be doing while I am trying to do what I am supposed to is akin to "rubbernecking" while driving. You know you need to pay attention to your surroundings, but part of you is drawn to the visual of the accident in the other lane. If I don't focus on my driving, I can cause yet another accident. What business is it of mine what happened over there? I need to pay attention to what *I* am doing and shoot up a quick prayer on behalf of the accident victims, their families, and their finances. Likewise, when I was supposed to focus on what I was doing and looked over I found myself being critical of what she was doing (or not doing) and would sometimes wonder, *Why should I bother doing any of this?* When my situation was not changing in any positive way, I often felt my effort was a waste of time. Instead of a reward, I got more of what the marriage didn't need—frustration and impatience. I finally realized that every one of us has a race to run and is responsible for his or her own actions. I said to myself, "Dude! Keep your eyes on the road ahead!" I only needed to say it once—maybe twice, definitely no more than a handful of times—and I have not done any rubbernecking since. Excuse me but I told you earlier and I was being honest, I am just a regular guy who's moving onto higher heights in God.

As men, we need to get to a place where we can say to ourselves and to other brothers in their times of need, "Just do your part in this. Trust God and he will do his part." What our wives do (or not do) has no impact on what God requires from his men. In recapping the commands charged to husbands, read the following out loud so that you hear it. It is purposefully repetitive helping to underscore the key points:

1. I am to become one with my wife.
   Q. Does knowing her role change what I am charged with?

2. I must fulfill her physical and emotional needs.
   Q. Does knowing her role change what I am charged with?

3. I should remain married despite the challenges.
   Q. Does knowing her role change what I am charged with?

4. If married to an unbeliever who accepts my faith, I should stay married to her.
   Q. Does knowing her role change what I am charged with?

5. As the husband, I am to be the head of my home.
   Q. Does knowing her role change what I am charged with?

6. I must love my wife as Christ loves the church.
   Q. Does knowing her role change what I am charged with?

7. I must love my wife as I love myself.
   Q. Does knowing her role change what I am charged with?

8. I should not treat my wife with embitterment.
   Q. Does knowing her role change what I am charged with?

9. I must remain faithful to my wife.
   Q. Does knowing her role change what I am charged with?

10. I must show my wife understanding and honor.
    Q. Does knowing her role change what I am charged with?

The resounding answer to the question is this: Regardless of whether she makes the job easy or makes it difficult, the charges still remain. With that, I concluded that adding her responsibilities in this book would be unwise. As you walk this assignment out, I am confident you will come to the same conclusion.

But is all of this really necessary? The saying is, happy wife, happy life. You know, I think that is what the serpent said to Adam in the garden. It worked with him, so he used it again with Abram—and Samson and Ahab and Herod . . . I think you get the picture. At every moment, as godly men we need to make sure "happiness" complies with God's commands. We will be accountable for every decision we make.

It definitely is true that both believers and unbelievers have had countless successful marriages alike. I never intended to imply that a couple cannot find happiness together without adhering to God's blueprint for marriage. What I *am* saying is this: It is not possible to have a bad marriage if both husband and wife are operating in the will of God. And, if husbands operate in the will of God, he is being obedient and there is blessing in that. It is just as important to note that operating in the will of God comes with incredible power. This power does not come from marriage itself but from God operating miraculously on our behalf because of our obedience.

A very good friend of mine reminded me of this: "One of you routs a thousand, because the Lord your God fights for you, just as he promised" (Joshua 12:10 NASB). If one routs a thousand, how many can the two rout? Is this applicable only to the wars of Israel during Joshua and Caleb? I don't believe so. The Lord fought for them constantly, keeping his word, when they were obedient. It is a prevalent theme throughout the Old Testament but not limited to it. If God decisively defeated, demoralized and dispelled a thousand of his enemies then, imagine what he will do for a husband and wife who are walking in his statues now.

I understand the obvious inconsistency I present. On the one hand I say this book is for men/husbands and that a woman's responsibility is irrelevant. On the other hand I present ideas on what the marriage might look like if the two are walking together in obedience to God— his ordinances. Here is the simple truth, as we have seen throughout this book: His blessing isn't contingent on the two walking in obedience. There are many blessings that come from our obedience alone. I also believe that if we are in it to win it, our wives will likely follow suit as they see the changes and their associated blessings.

Whenever God gave commands directly to people, steadfast obedience, immeasurable sacrifice, and dependence on God were essential. Today we won't stop overeating or going out with the boys and ogling women. We won't treat each other with respect, care for one another—the homeless, orphans, and widows. We won't even control our own thoughts and tongues. How is it conceivable that we would step out in faith by following a considerably more difficult command given directly to us by God? If we don't obey the little things, how can we expect that we would obey the larger ones? Many parts of life have gradations. In the video gaming world it is called "leveling up." In our walk with God, his expectation for us is that we level up. We must desire to level up!

There is *one* thing I do know about us. Dudes love a challenge—any kind of challenge. Am I right? I can think back to many ill-advised things I did just because someone challenged me. It is only because of God that I am alive and able to tell you about it. I can easily recall the many things I did only because someone said, "I betcha can't!" We were built to take on challenges and come out conquerors. My challenge to you is this: to look at your marriage as God sees it, to surrender your thoughts for his thoughts, your ways for his ways, and your speech for his speech. "I betcha can't!" Actually, I want you to know that I believe you can.

Single guys, this is what you have to look forward to, and I don't mean that in the same way that your regret-filled friend does. You can get yourself ready by preparing mentally, emotionally, and spiritually. Start by loving others the God kind of way in your inner circle, then outward to his people. Much like Jesus waiting for the Father to tell him it is time to go get his bride (the church), he will tell you. Patience is key. If you do it before you're ready, as I did, you'll have a lot of catching up to do. You will be working on self while working on the marriage, using God's statutes. That way is not the easier way, this being my testimony. It's like going to college *after* getting married, starting a career, and having children. Yeah, I did that backwards too. It is much more challenging to do it in that order than it is to go to college right out of high school, when there are far fewer responsibilities (and seemingly more hours in a day).

Married men, God made you for this. No one else but *you* need to be convinced of this (if you are not yet). If you are in a tough place in your marriage, you must have hope and faith. Keep pressing. Think back to those days when you began courting her. Remember when it felt like an eternity when you were apart for a day or two? The anticipation of going to see her Saturday afternoon when it was only Monday morning? Do you remember the times when you could talk for hours on the phone and hated to end the call? Yes, there is nothing like the feeling of the first kiss or the first date and, yes, those feelings did eventually temper. But those were only feelings. Feelings evolve and this is a good thing just as are those memories.

But I really need you to get this: How you love your wife from that point in time until the end is about *experience*. Experience has far more strength and longevity than feelings. You have the power to make that last kiss, that last dance, that last date infinitely more incredible than their firsts if you live and love each new day as you've never done before. This is by design! If afforded the opportunity to say goodbye and reflect on all of the things you've done together over the years, it will be so much more than any first of anything can ever be. If not given the ability to say goodbye, the lasts still exist, whenever the last time happens to be. So make that "happened to be" as reasonably frequent as possible. If you haven't kissed her in days, go kiss her now. If you haven't held her close and danced with her in years, go to her and do it now. Leave all of the bad and let all the good flood the moment and make it a memory. I promise you that this moment, and every future moment (God willing) will be more impactful than the very first and the most recent last. If you are blessed with a tomorrow, find another memorable first and live it as if it were your last! Your marriage is not over. Do not live the rest of your days together but lonely, waiting to die. By reading this book, you are already on your mark! Don't wait for the gun! *Go!*

To the divorced man, been there, done that, and I burned that T-shirt, never to repeat that visit! Your situation now is like that of the single man. Prepare yourself should God send you someone else, though it may be the last thing on your mind at the moment. Some of the things we learned in this book are the same principles we are to apply to others we encounter. There you will find plenty of opportunity for practice. Hopefully, as with the single guys, you will focus on your relationship with God during this period. He is not going to send his daughter to you if you are not ready. Now, if you may feel that you want to go find her, I encourage you to be patient. God knows you need a helper and that she needs you too. He already knows who is suitable. In the interim, begin knocking down as many of those "walls" you can do on your own, or with the help of God, or that of a counselor. Those walls are problematic to relationships, and I am confident your last marriage and subsequent divorce created new walls.

> Now all has been heard; here is the conclusion of the matter: Fear God and keep his commandments, for this is the duty of all mankind. For God will bring every deed into judgment, including every hidden thing, whether it is good or evil. (Ecclesiastes 12:13–14 NIV)

Pray for me as I pray for you, that together we unleash the power of God in our lives and marriages and that through us he may be glorified before an unbelieving world.

REFERENCES

n.d. *"counterpart."*. https://www.merriam-webster.com/dictionary/counterpart.

Andriy. n.d. *What is Human Behavior: A Deep Dive into Our Actions and Reactions.* https://psychology.tips/what-is-human-behavior/.

2018. *APA Dictionary of Psychology.* April 19. https://dictionary.apa.org/dissonance-reduction.

Baker, Warren, ed. 1994. *The Complete Word Study Old Testament.* Chattanooga, TN: AMG Publishers.

Bandoim, Lana. 2024. *What Does the Appendix Do?* July 30. https://www.verywellhealth.com/what-does-the-appendix-do-5270731.

2022. *Barna:minute Does Having a Confidant Support Men's Relational Well-Being?* June 2. https://barna.gloo.us/videos/barna-minute-confidant.

Bevere, John. 2023. *The Awe of God.* Nashville: Thomas Nelson.

n.d. *bitter.* https://www.merriam-webster.com/dictionary/bitter.

n.d. *blueprint.* https://dictionary.cambridge.org/dictionary/english/blueprint.

Breines, Juliana. 2016. *Why You Have to Love Yourself First.* January 30. https://www.psychologytoday.com/us/blog/in-love-and-war/201601/why-you-have-love-yourself-first.

Cartwright, Mark. 2018. *Medieval Chivalry.* May 14. https://www.worldhistory.org/Medieval_Chivalry/.

Casabianca, Sandra Silva, and Robyn Russell. 2021. *What Is Marital Rape?* June 23. https://psychcentral.com/lib/marital-rape.

n.d. *Female sexual dysfunction.* https://www.mayoclinic.org/diseases-conditions/female-sexual-dysfunction/symptoms-causes/syc-20372549.

Gaba, Sherry. 2021. *How Narcissists Withhold Love to Control Their Partners.* May 11. https://www.psychologytoday.com/us/blog/addiction-and-recovery/202105/how-narcissists-withhold-love-control-their-partners.

Gunther, Randi. 2023. *Withholding: A Dangerous Saboteur of Love.* August 31. https://www.psychologytoday.com/us/blog/rediscovering-love/202308/withholding-a-dangerous-saboteur-of-love.

Haiken, Melanie. 2014. *More Than 10,000 Suicides Tied To Economic Crisis, Study Says.* June 12. https://www.forbes.com/sites/melaniehaiken/2014/06/12/more-than-10000-suicides-tied-to-economic-crisis-study-says/.

Holland, Kimberly. 2019. *Understanding Female Sexual Arousal Disorder.* May 8. https://www.healthline.com/health/female-sexual-arousal-disorder.

Lenz, Lyz. 2024. *Why we need to stop telling women to 'just get married'.* April 1. https://www.msnbc.com/opinion/msnbc-opinion/the-cut-marrying-older-man-rcna145625.

2014. *Marital Status.* https://www.pewresearch.org/religious-landscape-study/database/marital-status/.

Meyers, Seth. 2022. *3 Signs That Someone Has Become Bitter.* November 18. https://www.psychologytoday.com/us/blog/insight-is-2020/202211/3-signs-that-someone-has-become-bitter.

—. 2023. *How People Become Bitter and Resentful.* November 7. https://www.psychologytoday.com/intl/articles/202311/how-people-become-bitter-and-resentful.

—. 2019. *How to Understand and Handle Bitter People.* October 7. https://www.psychologytoday.com/us/blog/insight-is-2020/201910/how-understand-and-handle-bitter-people.

Moore, Marissa. 2023. *Can Sexual Withholding Affect Your Marriage?* June 20. https://psychcentral.com/relationships/the-real-problem-with-sexual-withholding-in-a-marriage.

Pasque, Lisa Speckhard. 2023. *The lingering effects of sexual trauma.* June 7. https://mcpress.mayoclinic.org/women-health/lingering-effects-of-sexual-trauma/.

n.d. *persevere.* https://www.merriam-webster.com/dictionary/persevere.

Phillips, Suzanne B. 2021. *Repairing Sexual Withholding in a Marriage.* March 8. https://www.psychologytoday.com/us/blog/speaking-about-trauma/202103/repairing-sexual-withholding-in-marriage.

Q.ai. 2022. *How Long Did The Great Recession Last In 2008?* October 19. https://www.forbes.com/sites/qai/2022/10/19/how-long-did-the-great-recession-last-in-2008/.

n.d. *reproach.* https://www.merriam-webster.com/dictionary/reproach.

n.d. *selfish.* https://www.merriam-webster.com/dictionary/selfish.

Smith, Kurt. 2023. *Is It Okay To Be Withholding Sex In A Marriage?* April 11. https://www.guystuffcounseling.com/counseling-men-blog/is-it-okay-to-be-withholding-sex-in-a-marriage.

Strong, James. 2001. *The New Strong's Expanded Exhaustive Concordance of the Bible Red-Letter Edition.* Nashville: Thomas Nelson Publishers.

Team, SingleCare. 2024. *Erectile dysfunction statistics 2024.* May 21. https://www.singlecare.com/blog/news/erectile-dysfunction-statistics/.

n.d. *vehement.* https://www.merriam-webster.com/dictionary/vehement.

Verrett, Bethany. 2023. *When and How Was the Bible Split into Chapters and Verses?* August 04. https://www.biblestudytools.com/bible-study/topical-studies/when-and-how-was-the-bible-split-into-chapters-and-verses.html.

ACKNOWLEDGEMENTS

Taryn and Tselan, your love and support inspires me to keep striving. You guys are amazing!

Mom and Dad, thank you for all that you continue to pour into me.

Edward, thank you for your encouragement, sacrifice, and dedication.

Max, your support and our exchanges are invaluable. You stretch me.

ABOUT THE AUTHOR

While married to Joyce for sixteen years, Timothy has served in various capacities—Deacon, teacher, ministry leader, men's group facilitator, and others. He's earned a Master and Doctor of Divinity and has CBT, REBT, and life coach certifications. He serves as a U-CAN mentor for young men in the community.

Printed in the United States
by Baker & Taylor Publisher Services